Algorithmic Architecture

To my Sun for shedding a ray of light

Algorithmic Architecture

Kostas Terzidis

AMSTERDAM • BOSTON • HEIDELBERG • LONDON • NEW YORK • OXFORD
PARIS • SAN DIEGO • SAN FRANCISCO • SINGAPORE • SYDNEY • TOKYO
ARCHITECTURAL PRESS IS AN IMPRINT OF ELSEVIER

Architectural
Press

Architectural Press is an imprint of Elsevier
Linacre House, Jordan Hill, Oxford OX2 8DP
30 Corporate Drive, Suite 400, Burlington, MA 01803, USA

First edition 2006

British Library Cataloguing in Publication Data
A catalogue record for this book is available from the British Library

Library of Congress Cataloguing in Publication Data
Control Number: 2006922982

ISBN 13: 978-0-7506-6725-8
ISBN 10: 0-7506-6725-7

For information on all Architectural Press publications
visit our web site at http://books.elsevier.com

Printed and bound in Great Britain
06   07   08   09   10   10   9   8   7   6   5   4   3   2   1

Working together to grow
libraries in developing countries

www.elsevier.com | www.bookaid.org | www.sabre.org

ELSEVIER   BOOK AID
International   Sabre Foundation

Contents

Foreword   vii

Prologue   xi

1. The strive to capture the elusive   1

2. The intricacy of the otherness   15

3. A brief history of algotecture   37

4. Scripts, algorithms, and other predicaments   65

5. Amphiboly   105

6. Periplocus   117

7. Epi(multi)logue   131

Index   157

Foreword

Algorithmic Architecture or the Computer as a Double?

What should be the exact scope of the computer's involvement with architectural design? This question has been present since the beginning of computer aided architecture. It played, of course, a fundamental role in the first reflections and experiments regarding a possible computed or cybernetic architecture in the 1950s and 1960s. It did not disappear with the advent of post-modernism. The latter's concern with the linguistic dimension of architecture and urban design and the possibilities of formal exploration offered by the computer went hand in hand[1]. It is only during the last decade, with the spectacular development of computer graphics and the fascination exerted by the strange forms, the blobs and others that began to float on the designers' screens that this question was momentarily suspended. Now that this fascination is beginning to fade, the issue is back with all its complexity. There is no better proof of it than *Algorithmic Architecture*, since this book is primarily addressing the problem both at a technical and at a philosophical level.

Typically, the positions regarding the role of the computer in architectural design fall into two categories. For many designers, the computer is just an advanced tool running programs that enable them to produce sophisticated forms and to control better their realization. For those designers, although the machine does alter significantly the nature of the architecture that is produced, it is not necessary or even desirable to enter into the details of its inner processes. Despite their claim to the contrary, the greatest part of the blob architects fall into this category. Kostas Terzidis belongs clearly to the other camp composed of those who think that it has become unavoidable to enter into the black box of programming in order to make a truly creative use of the computer. In this perspective, a large section of his book is devoted to the exploration of what the mastery of scripting techniques can bring to architecture.

More than these technical insights, the main interest of *Algorithmic Architecture* may very well lie in the relation it establishes between the detailed examination of the possibilities offered by the computer and more general interrogations, of a philosophical nature, on the design process.

One of Terzidis' fundamental tenets is that design is not properly an invention, the creation of something absolutely new. It should rather be considered as the result of an unveiling or a rediscovery process. There is something almost pre-Socratic, or, to take a reference closer to our time, neoclassical, in this conception of design as a kind of return to an existing state of things that has fallen into oblivion. The pre-Socratic perspective would be to consider after Empedocles or Parmenides that nothing comes out of nothing and that the new is just the extant seen from a different vantage point. Neoclassical aesthetics and design theory starts as for it from the assumption that the quest for beauty is about recapturing the fresh inspiration that prevailed at some point towards the origin of art, an inspiration that accounts for the enduring value of archetypes. Part of Terzidis' ambition lies precisely in rethinking some of architecture's most fundamental archetypes in the light provided by computation.

There is something both disturbing and stimulating in a conception of design centered on the unveiling or the rediscovery. The disturbance becomes even more profound when Terzidis tells us that we shouldn't consider the computer as an extension of the mind, but rather as a partner in the design process with fundamentally different aptitudes and ways to reason. The computer is the Other of the human mind, not its mirror. There, the possible points of reference are to be found rather in the first years of computer aided architecture, when pioneers like Nicholas Negroponte, the founder of the Massachusetts Institute of Technology Media Lab, were presenting the introduction of computing in the design process as a dialogue between partners or "associates"[2]. However, Terzidis' perspective differs because of its insistence on the radical otherness of the computer.

But is this radical otherness fundamentally different from the estrangement from ourselves we experience day after day in the midst of any creative process? Something comes out from a region of our mind that we generally don't know much about, something that is both intriguing and secretly familiar. Kostas Terzidis is probably right in underlining the resemblance between invention and recognition. Without this familiarity, the new would be literally unthinkable. Its newness is nevertheless the product of an interior estrangement somewhat comparable to the distance that separates us from the computer.

At that stage, one might argue that the algorithmic procedures of the machine still remain fundamentally different from the way we think. But there again, a closer examination reveals a more ambiguous situation. For our mind follows rules in order to avoid the excessive familiarity that might otherwise defuse the originality of the creative endeavor, and these rules are usually as constraining as the algorithmic procedures run by the computer. In other words, the otherness that Terzidis attributes to the machine is also present in ourselves, in the apparent opposition between the creative impulse and the set of rules that enable us to control it. Is this opposition real? We know that rules can trigger imagination and that spontaneity always obeys to some hidden principles. The dichotomy between the spontaneous and the regulated has more to do with a polarity than with a clear-cut separation between two opposite faculties. One part of our inner self is constantly escaping regulation while the other tends to function in an almost mechanical way. Towards the end of the eighteenth century, the father of the *Encyclopédie*, the French philosopher Denis Diderot, was already wondering up to what point the mind is unpredictable and to what extent it could be compared to a machine[3]. Two centuries later, we are still in the midst of this conundrum.

The genuine excitement that Kostas Terzidis' book provokes might very well have to do with the perspectives he offers on this fundamental question. What if the radical other revealed by the computer was actually inside us, waiting for the machine to actualize it? If such was the case the computer might very well be more like a mirror showing us a reflection or a possible double of ourselves than a creature from another world. One thing is sure; architecture always appears as a compromise between rules and their contrary. Its expressive power might very well have to do with the secret analogy between this hybrid status and the intimate nature of our creative process. Ultimately, Kostas Terzidis' *Algorithmic Architecture* is about this analogy. It is not a book on computer and architecture. It is a book on architecture.

Antoine Picon
Professor of the History of Architecture and Technology,
Graduate School of Design, Harvard University

Endnotes

[1]There is more generally a strong link between the perspectives opened by computation in architecture and the emergence of contemporary architectural theory; for further discussion, see A. J. Magalhaes Rocha, *Architecture Theory 1960-1980: Emergence of a Computational Perspective*, doctoral dissertation submitted to the MIT Department of Architecture, Cambridge, Massachusetts, 2004.

[2]See for instance N. Negroponte, "Towards a Humanism through Machines", in *Architectural Design*, September 1969, pp. 511-512.

[3]Cf. J. Proust, *Diderot et l'Encyclopédie*, Paris, Armand Colin, 1962.

Prologue

Computation is a term that differs from, but is often confused with, computerization. While computation is the procedure of calculating, i.e. determining something by mathematical or logical methods, computerization is the act of entering, processing, or storing information in a computer or a computer system[i]. Computerization is about automation, mechanization, digitization, and conversion. Generally, it involves the digitization of entities or processes that are preconceived, predetermined, and well defined. In contrast, computation is about the exploration of indeterminate, vague, unclear, and often ill-defined processes; because of its exploratory nature, computation aims at emulating or extending the human intellect. It is about rationalization, reasoning, logic, algorithm, deduction, induction, extrapolation, exploration, and estimation. In its manifold implications, it involves problem solving, mental structures, cognition, simulation, and rule-based intelligence, to name a few.

The dominant mode of utilizing computers in architecture today is that of computerization; entities or processes that are already conceptualized in the designer's mind are entered, manipulated, or stored on a computer system. In contrast, computation or computing, as a computer-based design tool, is generally limited. The problem with this situation is that designers do not take advantage of the computational power of the computer. Instead some venture into manipulations or criticisms of computer models as if they were products of computation. While research and development of software involves extensive computational techniques, mouse-based manipulations of 3D computer models are not necessarily acts of computation. For instance, it appears, from the current discourse, that mouse-based manipulations of control points on NURBS-based surfaces are considered by some theorists to be acts of computing[ii]. While the mathematical concept and software implementation of NURBS as surfaces is a product of applied numerical computation, the rearrangement of their control points through commercial software is simply an affine transformation, i.e. a translation.

Presently, an alternative choice is being formulated that may escape these dialectically opposed strategies: algorithmic architecture. It involves the designation of software programs to generate space and form from the rule-based logic inherent in architectural programs, typologies, building code, and language itself. Instead of direct programming, the codification of design intention using scripting languages available in 3D packages (i.e. Maya Embedded Language (MEL), 3dMaxScript, and FormZ) can build consistency, structure, coherency, traceability, and intelligence into computerized 3D form. By using scripting languages designers can go beyond the mouse, transcending the factory-set limitations of current 3D software. Algorithmic design does not eradicate differences but incorporates both computational complexity and creative use of computers. For architects, algorithmic design enables the role of the designer to shift from "architecture programming" to "programming architecture." Rather than investing in arrested conflicts, computational terms might be better exploited by this alternative choice. For the first time perhaps, architectural design might be aligned with neither formalism nor rationalism but with intelligent form and traceable creativity.

Contrary to common belief, the word *algorithm* is not Greek[iii]. Its origin is Arabic, based on a concept attributed to an 8th century Persian mathematician named Al-Khwarizmi. An algorithm is a procedure for addressing a problem in a finite number of steps using logical if-then-else operations. In contrast, the word *allo* is indeed Greek and is the root of the word *else*, *alter*, and *other* which means that we do not know where it came from, foreign, strange, bizarre, odd, or perhaps, best, alien. To stretch even further the word *allo* can be associated with the a-logical. Yet, just because something is referred to as illogical it does not mean that it may not have its own internal logic, foreign though and perhaps incomprehensible for those outside of it. In a metaphorical sense, *allo* reminds us of an anecdote of a man sitting on one side of a river and asking somebody on the other side "how do I get to the other side?" And the other person responds "you *are* on the other side."

As the current theoretical discourse in architecture seems to elude around digital phenomena, a crucial critical discussion is emerging as a means to address, understand, clarify, and assess the elusive nature of this discourse. Issues related to virtuality, ephemerality, continuity, materiality, or ubiquitousness, while originally invented to explain digital or computational phenomena, are utilized today in the context of a traditionally still material-based architecture. What is the nature of their use? Is materiality subject to abstract digital concepts? What is (or is not) important?

The purpose of this book is to foster the dialogue about digital design, media, and technology and to challenge the basis of contemporary digital design arguments. The intention is to identify, distinguish, and offer a critique for current trends, tendencies, and movements in digital culture. Through diverse views it intends to develop a direction of thought into a proposed framework to sustain discourse that will challenge what is rapidly becoming the mainstream.

The structure of this book does not follow a traditional theory-based philosophical book format. It is not a computer programming/language tutorial book either. Even though there is a series of design work illustrated, it is not a design/graphics art book per se. Following the tradition of architecture as a conglomeration of various design fields, engineering, theory, art, and recently computation, the challenge of this book is to present a concept that, like architecture, is a unifying theme for many diverse disciplines. An algorithm is not only a computer implementation, a series of lines of code in a program, or a language, it is also a theoretical construct with deep philosophical, social, design, and artistic repercussions. Consequently, the book presents many, various, and often seemingly disparate points of view that lead to the establishment of one common theme which is the title of the book.

The first chapter is a trace back to the origin of design as a conceptual activity. It is based on an alternative definition of design, that of *schedio*, a Greek word that instead of pointing towards the future to where design is supposed to be materialized, it strangely points backwards in time where primitive archetypes are awaiting to be discovered. This reversion serves the purpose of defending a pre-Socratic philosophical position that claims that "nothing comes out of nothing and nothing disappears into nothing," indirectly negating the existence of novelty, a concept upon which modern design is based. In this chapter a critical standpoint is developed that seeks to assess the value of origin, archetype, and memory during the conceptual phase of design.

The second chapter seeks to identify, define, assess, and criticize a strange concept that emerges in computational processes, that of otherness. Introduced originally as an inversion of the traditional inference mechanism "if-then," this mechanism uses the alternative "else" as its point of departure. In doing so, it seeks to define the inconceivable, impossible, or unknown, concepts that by definition are out of the sphere of human understanding. Similarly, the notions of randomness, complexity, or infinity, arise as discrete quantifiable algorithmic processes that can be codified, implemented, and tested using computers. In this chapter, a conceptual framework is sought as the means to address design issues.

The third chapter is a historical and critical perspective on the recently emerging area of algorithms in architecture. It is differentiated from CAD or computer graphics in the sense that algorithmic processes are not necessarily based on computers. The questions that arise in this chapter are mainly associated with a historical overview and criticism of successes, pitfalls, and misunderstandings of the use of computation in design and architecture. Another interesting theme in this chapter is the comparative analysis between tool makers and tool users in the field of design.

Chapter 4 is a brief tutorial that introduces, explains, and articulates the use of scripting in architectural design. It starts with the basics of scripting, i.e. variables, arithmetic and logical operations, data structures, attributes, and procedures, and then progresses into more complex algorithms that have a high potential value in design: Boolean operations, stochastic search, fractals, cellular automata, and morphing. For each algorithm code, explanations, and examples are given. The purpose of this chapter is to show, clarify, and demystify the creation of algorithms and to provide some core examples that can be used as paradigms in different contexts.

The next two chapters, 5 and 6, are both illustrations of architectural design work that use algorithms, some of which were introduced in Chapter 4. The themes addressed are hybrid, synergistic, and poetic because the purpose here is to show a combined logic between humans and computers.

Chapter 5 is titled *Amphiboly* and it seeks to illustrate notions of ambiguity, ambivalence, and equivocation using computational schemes. The purpose is to investigate the possible ways that certain unique human characteristics can be expressed through algorithmic synthesis of forms. Three projects are presented: a parasite structure, a morphed high-rise, and a Boolean concert hall.

Chapter 6 is titled *Periplocus*, a Greek word that denotes an artificial complexity that is not based on quantitative means. The purpose is to show how intricate structures can emerge from simple algorithms whose beauty lies not in the complexity of the output or the number of lines in the code but rather in the articulation of a few elements in intricate ways. Three projects are presented: a subtle repetitive pattern for a house of worship, a stochastic-based residential high-rise, and a library generated out of its program.

Finally, the last chapter is a stream of thoughts, reactions, and criticisms on the ideologies developed in this volume. The discussion is presented in the format of an online multi-logue between the author and students of architecture, design, and media arts. A series of interesting thoughts emerge in the course of the discussion ultimately establishing a collective critical framework and challenging not only the author's positions but also the current mainstream discourse.

Endnotes

[i]In its colloquial sense, computerization refers to the process of furnishing with a computer or a computer system.

[ii]See Cuff, D., "Digital pedagogy: an essay: one educator's thoughts on design software's profound effects on design thinking and teaching," *Architectural Record*, September 2001. In this article, Cuff considers that computing is "one of the most important transformations of the contemporary profession" and that today "computing has become a populist skill."

[iii]If it were Greek it would have meant pain (algos). Algo-rithm would simply sound like the "rhythm of pain."

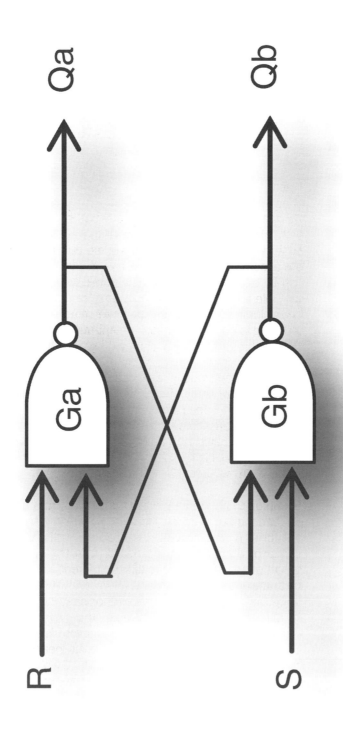

1 The strive to capture the elusive

Design is a term that differs from but is often confused with planning. While planning is the act of devising a scheme, program, or method worked out beforehand for the accomplishment of an objective, design is a conceptual activity of formulating an idea intended to be expressed in a visible form or carried into action. Design is about conceptualization, imagination, and interpretation. In contrast, planning is about realization, organization, and execution. Rather than indicating a course of action that is specific for the accomplishment of a task, design is a vague, ambiguous, and indefinite process of genesis, emergence, or formation of something to be executed but whose starting point, origin, or process is often uncertain. Design is about the spark of an idea and the formation of a mental image. It is about the primordial stage of capturing, conceiving, and outlining the main features of a plan and, as such, it always precedes the planning stage.

Etymologically, the verb *design* is derived from the prefix *de-* and the Latin verb *signare*, which means to mark, mark out, or sign. The prefix *de-* is used not in the derogatory sense of opposition or reversal but in the constructive sense of derivation, deduction, or inference. In that context, the word *design* is about the derivation of something that suggests the presence or existence of a fact, condition, or quality. In Greek, the word design is σχέδιο(pron. schedio), which is derived from the root σχεδὸν (pron. schedon), which means nearly, almost, about, or approximately. Thus, by its Greek definition, design is about incompleteness, indefiniteness, or imperfection, yet it is also about likelihood, expectation, or anticipation. In its largest sense, design signifies not only the vague, intangible, or ambiguous, but also the strive to capture the elusive[1].

Traveling further back into the origin of the Greek word σχεδόν (pron. schedon) one may find that it is derived from the word ἐσχειν (pron. eschein)[2] which is the past tense of the word ἔχω (pron. echo) which in English means to have, hold, or possess. Translating the etymological context into English, it can be said that design is about something we once had, but have no longer. The past tense in the Greek language is referred to as indefinite (αόριστος) and, as such, it is about an event that did occur at an unspecified time in the past, hence it could have happened any time between a fraction of a second and years ago. So, according to the Greeks, design is linked indirectly to a loss of possession and a search into an oblivious state of memory. This linguistic connection reveals an antithetical attitude towards design that, in the Western culture at least, is about stepping into the future, a search for new entities, processes, and forms, frequently expressed by the terms *novelty* or *innovation*. Before adventuring any further into this Greek paradox, it may be useful to examine the notion of innovation and novelty within the context of design, and specifically architectural design.

Innovation is a term amply used in association with the process or products of design. It is defined as "the act of beginning or introducing something for, or as if for, the first time." Surprisingly, there is something strange about the definition. It appears to be a semantic twist within the definition of innovation itself. It involves the conjugation "as if" which means literally "in the same way that it would be if" asserting the possibility of an equivalence between existence and the perception of existence. While the adjective "for" is a definite indicator that connects an object, aim, or purpose to an action or activity, the conjugation "as if" involves a hypothetical conjecture posed over the truthfulness of the statement. Such a definition is, to say the least, paradoxical, contradictory, and problematic in the sense that while the definition itself is supposed to lead towards a definite assertion, it involves also the possibility of negating the same assertion; if the assertion is that innovation is indeed about the first time then it is contradictory also to assume that such a uniqueness can also be perceived as such, because then it implies that something that may not be *first* may also be assumed, presented, or perceived as *first*, which is an apparent contradiction. In other words, the definition of innovation involves a possibility of a deliberate, unintentional, or accidental flaw: *if something is perceived as such then it must be such*. This syllogism brings up an important hypothesis about perception: that it is possible that something can be constructed to appear as such or that an audience may be conditioned to perceive something as such. In either case, the definition of innovation seems to suffer from the lack of two of the most fundamental principles of every definition: clarity and truthfulness.

Because of its pioneering nature, innovation is frequently associated with originality. Originality is defined as the quality or state of preceding all others in time. Innovation is also defined as the act of introducing something new, i.e. something that comes into existence for the first time. However, unlike innovation, originality is about a point of departure, a source of knowledge, an archetype, a primordial mark at which something comes into existence, an ancestral origin whose genetic material transcends throughout the following generations. Unlike innovation, the importance of originality is to be "first in order" and this quality is not a matter of perception but rather a matter of necessity. While the intention of both processes may be similar, their logical directions are antithetical. If innovation leads towards one direction, then the search for originality leads towards the opposite. Innovation may be seen as a process of adding one more leaf to the tree, whereas originality can be seen as the process of adding one more root.

In tracing back to the origin one is forced to travel from the leaves backwards towards the roots. This process involves at least two modes of thought: reduction and reversion. While the notion of reduction can be associated with decrement, lessening, or diminishment, it can also be associated with abstraction, simplification, and idealization. Similarly, reversion is about regression, setback, or recall, yet it can also be about return, reassessment, and reconsideration. The reason for this is that the prefix *re-* is used not in the negative sense of backwards or regress, but rather in the positive sense of again or anew. Interestingly, the term *innovation* is commonly associated with progress, advancement, growth, and expansion, terms that ironically are also considered to be the opposites of reduction and reversion.

In architectural design, the notion of innovation has been a founding, axiomatic, and guiding principle. Within the modernist tradition of novelty, the search for innovation may have become a misguiding rather than a guiding factor in design. While *the shock of the new* may have provided in the early 20th century an escape from the traditions of the past, its constant use in the world of fashion today and the everlasting struggle to introduce something new for, or as if for, the first time defies its original purpose. Novelty is a primordial fascination of the human mind, yet its perception seems to be highly illusory, conditioned, and influenced. As Wes Jones points out, "we believe that newer is better. Not because it is a fact in each individual case, but because it is an inevitability in general." While many theorists are concerned with the value of newness, it may also be useful to explore the question of "what is new?" Just because something appears to be new or is labeled as new, it does not mean that it is *essentially* new. Like a magician's show, the appearance or disappearance of objects in a scene generates a primordial fascination from the viewpoint of the audience; yet not from the magician's viewpoint[3]. Novelty requires more than just appearance. As in the case of innovation versus originality, novelty is usually about the striking, different, or unusual but it can also be about the first, seminal, or original. A difference in appearance does not necessarily justify novelty. If something is seen from a different angle, is rotated upside down, or a piece is added that does not mean that the result is new, yet it may appear to be as if new. In contrast, an original concept involves newness in a productive, seminal, and influential way.

As mentioned earlier, the notion of design, according to the Greeks, is associated with the past instead of the future. Such an assumption appears almost antithetical to the predominant notion of design as a process that leads towards the derivation of novelty. How can the past be of such significant importance, especially as a recollection of past lost thoughts? If, according to the Greeks, design is about something that we had but do not have any more, hence it is lost somewhere in the past, what is its connection to something that is about to become the future, i.e. a novelty? Why would they bring up such an unexpected and obscure relationship? Is it possible that novelty in the sense that we understand it today, according to the Greeks, does not exist per se and anything new is just *an illusion*?

If we look deeper into pre-Socratic philosophers such as Xenophanes, Parmenides, or Zeno, one of the common agreements between them was the assumption that nothing comes out of nothing and nothing disappears into nothing; nothing can just pop up or vanishes without a trace. Such an assumption is very important to understand their reluctance to conceive, accept, or understand the concept of novelty in its modern sense. If everything is indestructible then change is nothing but a transformation from one state into another; the appearance or disappearance of parts is only phenomenal; nothing is added or subtracted. Therefore, if something emerges, appears, or claims to be new, then it must be nothing but an illusion, because if it is not, then it would contradict the initial premise of preservation. Such logic, while it may appear to be simplistic or absolute, is also very powerful because it does not allow thoughts to be affected by sensory phenomena. What is most significant about this logic is that it sets a paradigm in which knowledge about reality is based upon reason and therefore strives to be truthful, while human opinion of appearance is based upon our senses, which are not only unreliable but also misleading[4]. According to this logic, design as a mental process of creation can be seen as bounded by the limits of preservation: any newly conceived thought, process, or form is nothing but a reordering of previous ones. However, if we consider this possibility, then we are confronted with the problem of origin: as every "new" idea depends on its previous one, then there must be an origin, a starting point, a root or roots out of which everything spurs, tangles, and multiplies offering glimpses of what appears occasionally to be "new." Hence, we are led to the conclusion that the origin, like its material counterpart, must be fixed, eternal, and indestructible. And since novelty involves the negation of existence (i.e. something that did not exist before), novelty is impossible. It is only a sensory illusion[5].

In English, the word *existence* is derived from the prefix ex- (i.e. forth) and the verb *sistere*, which in Latin means to cause to stand up or come to a stop. Thus, etymologically the meaning of the word *existence* can be associated with the action of appearance or arising. In Greek, the word *existence* is ὑπαρξη which is derived from the prefix ὑπο (*hypo-*), i.e. under, below, or beneath, and the noun αρχή (*arche*), i.e. beginning, start, or origin[6]. Thus, similarly to design, existence is not only about the distant past, the beginning of things but also even further, as it involves a step beyond, below, or beneath the starting point. But how is that possible? How can something lay beyond the beginning? Wouldn't that result in a new beginning which then should be displaced again ad infinitum? Such a train of thoughts may appear paradoxical because it is interpreted as a sequential linkage in the context of a beginning and an ending point. As established earlier, in the pre-Socratic spirit, the notion of a beginning must be rejected (as well as that of an end). Things exist before their phenomenal starting point and therefore the use of the prefix *hypo-* declares the framework, structure, or platform out of which starting points can be observed. Similar to a river, its origin is not the spring itself but rather lies far beyond, beneath, or below its phenomenal emergence.

The verb *to become* is used in English to denote the action of coming into existence, emerging, or appearing. In language, as opposed to formal logic, existence is a predicate rather than a quantifier, and the passage from copulative to existential can be misleading. The action of coming-to-be or becoming does not necessarily have to be associated with creation, beginning, or emergence, but rather may denote a process of derivation, transformation, or transition from one state into another. Transition is indeed an act of becoming except its connotation is problematic because as Evans points out "whatever is subject to the transformation must already be complete in all its parts"[7] a notion antithetical to the traditional view of design as an accumulative process. For example, the subtraction of one point from a square may result in a triangle that, in turn, can be perceived as an action in which "a square became a triangle." In this case, the action of becoming results from an operation of subtraction. Furthermore, the action of subtraction itself is also an action of becoming where "a point became nothing." Such an action involves the existential operation of instant becoming. The pre-Socratic philosophers rejected such a notion as absurd, because nothing can just come into being or suddenly cease to exist. As they rejected traditional explanations for the phenomena they saw around them in favor of more rational explanations, they also set the limits of human imagination. According to Parmenides, if something came into being, it is not (εἰ γὰρ ἐγέντ', οὐκ ἐστιν), i.e. something that pops out of nothing, cannot really exist[8]. Not surprisingly, even today, there is no word in the English or, for that matter, Greek language that can denote the instant becoming of an object out of nothing. While the verb *to become* is the closest one, it implies a moment of time in order to originate. The same is true for the terms *emergence, genesis, birth, rise, derivation, start,* or *beginning* where time is always involved[9]. Similarly, the word *appearance* cannot be equivalent to the word *become* because it involves the subjective interpretation of the existence of an object. Appearance is about the visual interpretation of the existence of something that is coming into sight. Surprisingly, the most common word used by people to denote sudden appearance or disappearance is the word *magic*, but this also carries an illusionary, unreal, perhaps deceptive connotation. A connotation associated with the belief that it is the result of a supernatural event.

It can be argued that coolness, fashion, style, the unapologetically fashionable, desirable, and ephemeral[10], are not about the new but instead are deceptive obfuscating methods of establishing an authority on art, architecture, and design without offering the means to truly lead towards novelty. In contrast, theories, experiments, or technologies that point out the potential limits of the human mind, seek to identify novelty as a quality that exists beyond the limits of the human mind. If there is novelty, in the existential sense, it must be sought beyond, below, or beneath its phenomenal appearances as an already existing entity that is out of human knowledge.

Novelty therefore must be the result of discovery. While knowledge about the lack of existence is impossible, the lack of knowledge about existence is possible. In other words, the discovery of the existence of something is indeed new, as it pertains to the body of knowledge that it adds to. It is about the existence of something that was, until it was discovered, out of the set of human knowledge. Unlike mere compositional rearrangement of existing elements into seemingly new entities, a discovery is a revelation of something that existed before but was not known.

Discovery is the act of encountering, for the first time, something that already existed. In contrast, invention is defined as the act of causing something to exist by the use of ingenuity or imagination; it is an artificial human creation. Both discovery and invention are about the origin of ideas and their existence in the context of human understanding. These two intellectual mechanisms result from a logic, which tends to argue whether the existence of certain ideas, notions, or processes is one of the following: either a human creation or simply a glimpse of an already existing universe regardless of the presence of humans. The most paradigmatic example of this polemic is that of geometry itself: the existence of geometry can be regarded as either a descriptive revelation of properties, measurements, and relationships of existing forms or as an arbitrary, postulate-based mental structure that exists only in the human mind. For instance, Euclidean geometry was developed originally to measure distances on the surface of earth and yet, in Euclidean geometry, platonic primitive shapes, such as squares, circles, or triangles, do not exist per se in nature yet they represent idealized approximations of natural objects. Likewise, architecture can be regarded as either a simulation of the laws and structure of nature or as a world of fantasy and imagination[11].

The notion of an origin is important when discussing the process of design. Because of its investigative nature design is always associated with a starting point, a pivot, out of which style, fashion, or mannerisms result. That starting point is important for at least two reasons: first, and most obvious, it serves as a pivotal point of reference that identifies, categorizes, and determines a wide range of similar products. Second, and less obvious, is the fact that an origin belongs to the distant past and as such it involves the reminiscence of something that was lost but whose consequences are still present. While memory is usually about mundane, common, and ordinary past events, it is also about that which is lost in the distant past, the primordial, archaic, and primitive. The origin, as such, is elusive, evasive, and indefinite yet it is always present in the form of a sign that points out at the increasingly distant past. While the struggle to seek for the latest new *new thing* may be fascinating, seductive, or thrilling, it is only because it builds upon a primordial human weakness, that of the vulnerable nature of the senses. In contrast, the search for original, universal, and ideal forms of existence which serve as prototypes, archetypes, or models is a glimpse into an already existing world whose rules adhere to entirely different principles of those that govern the world of senses.

Thus, in searching for the origin one is challenged to seek the basic, archaic, and primitive qualities of the first encounter. The process of recollection is a search for the truth, whereas the act of concealing will eventually lead to false assumptions[12]. The search for truth leads to facts that will be remembered for a long time while falsity leads to facts that, while impressive at the moment, will pass into oblivion. Memory is an associative mechanism for reproducing past experiences and in its primitive neural level it is governed by logical operations. Yet, while the primitive connections that reproduce a past event may be logical, the higher level entities that are to be remembered are not necessarily so.

Memory relies on a concept called feedback, that is, the output of something being fed back into itself as input. The minimal definition of a feedback involves at least two consecutive moments of time as a measure of comparison is established so that an event can be locked and therefore be "remembered." In electronics, the basic element for storing binary information is termed a *flip-flop*. It is composed of two cross-coupled NOR gates, as shown in Figure 1.1. If R and S are opposites of one another, then Qa follows S and Qb is the inverse of Qa. However, if both R and S are switched to 0 simultaneously, then the circuit will return what was previously presented on R and S. Hence this simple logical circuit constitutes a memory element, or a flip-flop that locks or "remembers" which of the two inputs S and R was most recently equal to one[13].

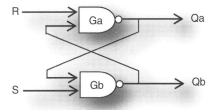

1.1
A flip-flop

S	R	Qa	Qb
0	0	0/1	1/0
0	1	0	1
1	0	1	0
1	1	0	0

1.2
Truth table

Time is therefore "captured" by reversing its order so that an event can be revisited. The configuration of a memory unit can be illustrated as a geometrical relationship where two parallel lines are connected by establishing a cross-coupled zigzag path. This simple geometrical relationship reveals a strange paradox: while "before" always knows what comes after, "after" never knows what lies before it. In other words, in order to know what will happen, one needs to be where nobody can go, i.e. in the future. However, future is relative to where the past starts. If the future of one observer is observed from the past of another observer, then the past of the first observer becomes the future of the second. Time therefore can be reversed momentarily to collect fragments of time that are called memories.

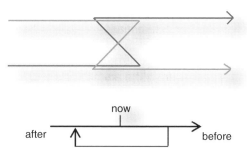

1.3
Feedback (below) and a cross-coupled zigzag path (above)

Symbolically, according to the Greeks, it was Chronos (Time) who ruled first and what was produced, the children of Time, were devoured by time. It was only when Time was conquered and an origin was set to its passing. That origin, the origin of human thinking, was established out of the emergence of two newly acquired fundamental abilities: that of memory (attributed to Epimetheus) and that of prediction (attributed to Prometheus). As a consequence, it was the realization of the inevitability of death that initiated history, i.e. the preservation of memory and the explanation of time as a passing phenomenon. The ability to make logical syllogisms, i.e. to see the connection between the notions of before and after is one of the main characteristics that distinguish intellectually humans from animals. Without logic there is no ability to foresee events and therefore make sense out of time. One moment has meaning only in its relation to other moments: otherwise they are just fragments deprived of meaning if they are not related to other fragments. Historically, as the distinction between the emotional and logical side of the primitive human mind started to become clearer, humans started to differentiate their nature from that of animals. Hybrid creatures that exist in various mythologies such as the Minotaur, Sphinx, Centaur, or Medusa, represent a symbolic struggle to identify, differentiate, and demarcate human nature from that of animals establishing its superiority through slaughter. George Bataille in his work *Le Labyrinthe* offers a deeply existential interpretation of the diacritical couple man/animal and the desire to set free man's animality. According to Hollier's interpretation, in Lascaux's caves Bataille sees as the origin of painting the desire of man to represent his triumph over the animal and not as a Narcissisian pictorial urge[14]. Similarly, in *Aesthetics*, Hegel interprets Oedipus' answer to Sphinx's riddle as man's answer that eliminates any trace of animality, an answer that makes "know thyself" the unique and differentiating principle that identifies the human species. Parmenides' distinction between truth and opinion is both evangelism and warning as it sets a departing point away from the animal logic and identifies a new path of truth but at the same time warns that this newly discovered world will be hunted by the other logic it leaves behind.

The primitive, eternal, and universal nature of archetypes serves not only as a point of departure but also as a point of reference. Aldo Rossi refers to this nature as archaic, unexpressed, and analogical[15]. Yet, he also made a distinction between history and collective memory. As the relationship between form and function erodes over time there is a disjunction in meaning that results in a twist in the flow of history: where history ends, memory begins[15]. The form empty of meaning engulfs its own individuality and stands alone, away, orphaned, and rootless. Yet, it is then that remembrance becomes the only way back. Ironically, souvenir is about the act of remembering and yet, it is only by forgetting that one can see again things as they really are; the act of forgetting is not a submersion into oblivion but rather the erasure of false connections and the return to the umbilical origin.

Endnotes

[1]Precisely, the root of σχεδόν (pron. schedon) is derived from ἐσχειν (pron. eschein), which is the past tense of the verb ἔχω (pron. eho), that is, to have. Therefore, design literally is about the reminiscence of a past possession at an indefinite state and at an uncertain time. Similarly, the word *scheme*, from the Greek σχῆμα, means shape and is also derived from the root σχεδόν.

[2]εσχειν (pron. eschein) is also the root of the English word scheme.

[3]Similarly, in the game of peek-a-boo a baby is mysteriously fascinated by an appearing/disappearing face.

[4]The Socratic analogy to shadows in a cave illustrates the illusion-prone nature of the senses and the inability to distinguish reality (light) from its representation (shadow). The feeling of sensory illusion is so comfortable that attempts to reveal its deceptive nature is met with fierce resistance (Republic, book VII). While in Plato's dialogue *Parmenides* there is a clear distinction between the Socratic theory of ideas and Parmenides' existential philosophy, both are in agreement on the deceptive nature of the senses.

[5]To paraphrase a paradox by Zeno, a student of Parmenides, it can be argued that novelty resembles an arrow moving forward in time and as a moving arrow either it is where it is or it is where it is not. If it is where it is, then it must be standing still, and if it is where it is not, then it can't be there; thus, it cannot change position. Of course, the paradox is just a symbolism of the inability to achieve something out of nothing, i.e. to create something new.

[6]Alternative versions of the word ὑπαρξη (i.e. *existence*) in Greek are υπόστασῃ which is equivalent to *ex-sistere* and τοωντι, which literally means, *this which is*. Όν (pron. on), which is the root of the word ontology, is the present participle of the verb ειμί (i.e. *I am*).

[7]See Evans, R., "Not to be used for wrapping purposes", AA Files, vol. 10, 1985, p. 70. In this article Evans makes an elegant distinction between design as an accumulative process and transformation as a different type of design where only relations alter.

[8]Along the line of pre-Socratic thought, the prefixes a-, un- or in-, when used in the sense of negation, opposition, or contrast to reality, are absurd, confusing, and pointless. Either something exists or it does not. The preposterousness that is inherent in the negation of existence is very apparent in two linguistic constructions namely the words *unknown* and *unreal*. Both are terms that while they exist as words they are both preposterous.

[9]Beginnings and endings represents change and transitions such as the progression of past to future, of one condition to another, of one vision to another, and of one universe to another. New or

old do not have existence of their own but rather are seen as transitions from one state to another.

[10]Amongst other theorists, Lavin claims that contemporary architecture should seek for ephemeral qualities that will give modernity a fashionable "new look." She praises superficial qualities such as lamination, decoration, or coloration to be catalysts that will signify the contemporary; in her words "better now than forever". See Lavin S. "In a Contemporary Mood" in Hadid Z and P. Schumacher (eds.) *Latent Utopias* Wien: Springer-Verlag, 2002, pp. 46-7.

[11]Perault, the architect of the peristyle of the Louvre, argued that architecture is a fantastic art of pure invention. He asserted that architecture really exists in the mind of the designer and that there is no connection to the natural world. In addition, architecture as an imaginative art, obeys its own rules which are internal and personal to each designer, and that is why most creators are vaguely aware of the rules of nature and yet produce excellent pieces of art. A similar point is also argued by Giovanni Battista Vico. In his work *The New Science* (1744), Vico argues that one can know only by imagining. The twisting of language and meaning can lead one to discover new worlds of fantasy. He argued that one can know only what one makes. Only God can understand nature, because it is his creation. Humans, on the other hand, can understand civilization, because they made it. The world of civil society has certainly been made by men, and its principles are therefore to be found within the modification of our own human mind.

[12]In Greek the word *false* is λάθος(pron. lathos) which is derived from the word λήθη which means oblivion. In contrast, the word *truth* is αλήθεια (pron. aletheia) which is derived from the negating prefix a- and the word λήθη, therefore denoting the negation to forget. Thus, the connection is that truth is unforgettable and falsity is oblivious; or rather that truth leads to facts that will be remembered for a long time while falsity leads to facts that, while impressive at the moment, will pass into oblivion. The word λήθη is translated by Heidegger as *concealment* therefore reinterpreting the act of forgetting as one "sunk away into concealedness." See Heidegger, M., *Parmenides*, Bloomington: Indiana University Press, 1992, p. 71.

[13]See Hamacher, C., Vranesic, Z., and Zaky, S., *Computer Organization*. New York: McGraw-Hill, 1984, pp. 520–521.

[14]See Bataille, G., *Visions of Excess: Selected Writings,* 1927–1939, A. Stoekl (ed.). Minneapolis: University of Minnesota Press, 1985, pp. 171–177. See also Hollier, D., *Against Architecture: The Writings of Georges Bataille.* Cambridge: MIT Press, 1989, pp. 57–73.

[15]See Rossi, A., "An Analogical Architecture". *Architecture and Urbanism 56* (May 1976). Also in Nesbitt, K. (ed.), *Theorizing a New Agenda for Architecture*. New York: Princeton Architectural Press, 1996, pp. 348–352.

[16]See Rossi, A., *The Architecture of the City*. Cambridge: MIT Press, 1984, p. 7.

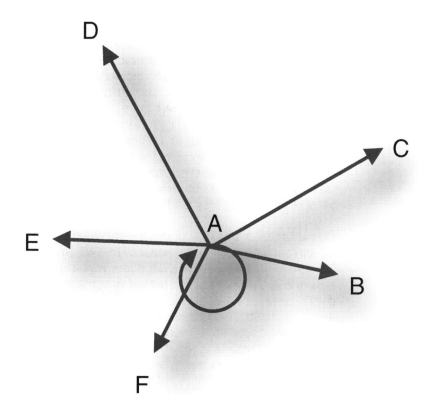

2 The intricacy of the otherness

An algorithm is a process of addressing a problem in a finite number of steps. It is an articulation of either a strategic plan for solving a known problem or a stochastic search towards possible solutions to a partially known problem. In doing so, it serves as a codification of the problem through a series of finite, consistent, and rational steps. While most algorithms are designed with a specific solution in mind to a problem, there are some problems whose solution is unknown, vague, or ill-defined. In the latter case, algorithms become the means for exploring possible paths that may lead to potential solutions.

Theoretically, as long as a problem can be defined in logical terms, a solution may be produced that will address the problem's demands. An algorithm is a linguistic expression of the problem and as such it is composed of linguistic elements and operations arranged into spelling, and grammatically and syntactically correct statements. The linguistic articulation serves the purpose not only to describe the problem's steps but also to communicate the solution to another agent for further processing. In the world of computers, that agent is the computer itself. An algorithm can be seen as a mediator between the human mind and the computer's processing power. This ability of an algorithm to serve as a translator can be interpreted as bi-directional: either as a means of dictating to the computer how to go about solving the problem, or as a reflection of a human thought into the form of an algorithm. The latter one will be addressed in more detail later in this chapter.

Traditionally, algorithms were used as mathematical or logical mechanisms for resolving practical problems. With the invention of the computer, algorithms became frameworks for implementing problems to be carried out by computers. While the connotation associated with the action of giving instructions, commands, or directions is subconsciously assumed to be aimed at a sentient worker, the computer, despite its once human identity, is not a human being and therefore should not be treated as such. (Perhaps it would be more accurate if a new name was given that would reflect more accurately its true potential, such as portal, transverser, or, hyperion[1].) By liberating the user of a computer from material concerns associated with labor, skill, or complexity or from emotional factors such as compassion, fatigue, or boredom computers can be utilized as tireless vehicles that allow humans to realize, overcome, and ultimately surpass their own physical and mental limitations. The significance of this liberation lies not that much in the amount of work that can be accomplished but rather in the fact that the human mind is in a position to invent devices that will help it exceed its own limitations. Furthermore, through such inventions such as the computer a world is encountered, that of applied computation, which, while intellectual in nature, abides to principles, mechanisms, and performances that lie beyond the realm of the human mind.

An algorithm is a set of instructions given by a human to be performed by a computer. Therefore, an algorithm can describe either the way a problem is to be addressed as if it would be resolved by a human or the way it should be addressed to be understood by a computer (the notion of "understanding" here refers to the capacity the computer has to process information given by a human and not to its conscious interpretation of that information).

In taking the first case, an algorithm becomes a rationalized version of human thinking. As such it may be characterized as being precise, definite, and logical, but at the same time may also lack certain unique qualities of human expression such as vagueness, ambiguity, or ambivalence. While this may be true as far as the linguistic expression is concerned, it is not necessarily true for the products of the language. For instance, one can use unambiguous words to articulate an ambiguous statement, i.e. "the man saw the monkeys in his pyjamas." In other words, the explicit nature of the statements that compose an algorithm do not necessarily also reflect the explicit nature of the output. Likewise, precise platonic geometrical shapes can be combined algorithmically to produce quite ambiguous geometrical forms. Just because the language elements or even the syntax is rational, it does not mean that the products will also follow the same trend i.e., to be rational.

In the second case, an algorithm is seen as a linguistic expression fitted to the needs of the computer. As such it becomes an idiomatic language of conformity or adaptation to an alien reasoning. The word *alien* is used here not as a means of intimidation but rather as an indicator of an alternative, perhaps parallel, logic to that employed by the human mind. Contrary to common belief, a computer's logic, while seemingly a product of the human mind, is not a subset of it but rather a parallel, if not superset, to it. When inputting information in the form of an algorithm for a computer to process, one must adjust one's reasoning to the reasoning of the computer-worker and not to that of a human-worker. Certain qualities of the human mind such as those that contribute to what is considered "smart," i.e. sharpness, quick thought, or brightness, may not be desirable or even applicable when dealing with the computer's reasoning. What is considered to be smart in one world may be considered dumb in another world; this is precisely the reason why the two reasoning systems are parallel, complementary, or perhaps antithetical. For instance, to find a secret password a human may exploit context-based conjectures, reductive reasoning, assumptions, or even spying as strategies for saving time and effort. In contrast, a computer can solve the same problem by simply checking all possible combinations of all alphanumeric symbols until a match is found. Such a strategy, referred to as brute force, would be considered overwhelming, pointless, naïve, or impossible by a human investigator. Nonetheless, given the computational power of a computer such a strategy may only take a few seconds to check millions of possibilities, something inconceivable to the human mind.

The term *inconceivable* is used here to denote an inability to comprehend, and implicitly it refers to the human mind. Clearly, the term is figurative, metaphorical, or linguistic, for if it were literal it would contradict itself as a paradox: how could one conceive that which cannot be conceived? In the pre-Socratic spirit, the negation of something negates its own existence[2]. While it is possible to construct a word signifying a negation or an impossibility it does not mean that what is signified also exists, at least in the sense of being actual as opposed to fictional, predicative, or identificatory. So, to say that something was inconceivable to the human mind means that a now perceived as possible thought would not have occurred to the human mind before. However, within the world of computation the boundaries of impossibility are yet to be defined. The power of computation, which involves vast quantities of calculations, combinatorial analysis, randomness, or recursion, to name a few, point out to new "thought" processes that may have not ever occurred to the human mind. These "idea generators" which are based on computational schemes have a profound ability not only to expand the limits of human imagination but also to point out the potential limitations of the human mind. What was inconceivable once may have been so mainly because it may have escaped the possibility of existence.

Similarly, the term *impossible* is used here to denote the incapability of having existence or of occurring. Yet, the boundaries beyond which possible starts to be perceived as impossible tend to change constantly in a world enhanced by computer-augmented human thinking. Even within the realm of the human mind those boundaries seem to expand in a Guinness-wise fashion. For instance, recently the total number of digits of the constant number Pi memorized by a human mind is 83,431, held in 2005 by a 59-year-old Japanese person named Akira Haraguchi. At the same time Japan wants to develop a supercomputer that can operate at 10 petaflops, or 10 quadrillion (10,000,000,000,000,000 or 10^{16}) calculations per second, which is 35 times faster than the Blue Gene/L, the current US record holder with 280.6 teraflops – that is 280.6 trillion calculations a second, numbers thought to be astronomical a few years ago. Therefore, the boundaries of what is considered impossible may be shifting constantly based on real facts and not conjectures[3]. Where is the threshold beyond which something is impossible – or should we say the threshold below which something is possible? Theoretically, nothing is impossible. Even if it seems so at the moment, it may be that such a possibility has not yet arrived. The old proverb stated as "if you have all the time and all the resources in the world, is there anything you cannot do?" may indeed seem as a false premise yet it also defines the possibility of the impossible.

Contrary to common belief, algorithms are not always based on a solution strategy conceived entirely in the mind of a human programmer. Many algorithms are simulations of the way natural processes work and as such they must not be regarded as human inventions but rather as human discoveries. Unlike inventions, discoveries are not conceived, owned, or controlled by the human mind, yet as abstract processes they can be captured, codified and executed by a computer system. In this case, the human programmer serves the purpose of translating a process external to the human mind to be compiled into machine language which is also external to the human mind. For instance, a genetic algorithm is a process that simulates the behavior and adaptation of a population of candidate solutions over time as generations are created, tested, and selected through repetitive mating and mutation. The algorithm uses a stochastic search based on the chance that a best solution is possible and that computer processing power is effortless, rapid, and precise from the viewpoint of the human programmer. Yet, nothing in the entire algorithm is about human invention; the process is called natural selection (a process occurring in nature regardless of the presence of humans) and the flow of the calculations is logical or arithmetic (both processes occurring in nature regardless of the presence of humans).

Interestingly, algorithms can generate other algorithms; not only precise, identical, multiple copies of themselves but also structured text (i.e. code) that when executed will behave as an algorithm. In fact, the process of composing an algorithm is also an algorithm in itself, that is, the algorithm that created the algorithm. This self-referential property (which may be referred to here as meta-algorithm, i.e. the algorithm of an algorithm) is important in design for at least two reasons: first, like algorithms, design can be seen as a set of procedures that lead stochastically towards the accomplishment of a goal. In studying the articulation of algorithms one may be able to discern similarities with design. While such a study may lead to the development of procedures that may be useful in design, more importantly, it may reveal certain clues about design as a mental process. This possibility opens up a more intricate relationship between design and algorithm than has been previously possible. Rather than using algorithms to copy, simulate, or replace manual methods of design (while perhaps desirable), instead they can be studied as methodologies that operate in ways similar, parallel, or complementary to that of the human mind. Second, along the lines of *homo faber homo fabricatus* (i.e. we make a tool and the tool makes us), algorithms can be seen as design tools that lead towards the production of novel concepts, ideas, or forms, which, in turn, have an effect in the way designers think thereafter. That way of thinking is incorporated in the next generation of tools that will, in turn, affect the next generation of designers, and so on.

It may be assumed that meta-algorithmics, that is, the creation of algorithms that generate other algorithms, is a human creation as well. A human programmer must have composed the first algorithm that, in turn, generates new algorithms and as such the initial programmer must be in control of the original idea. However, this is not necessarily true. Unlike humanly conceived ideas, where the author is the intellectual owner of the idea, algorithms are processes that define, describe, and implement a series of actions that in turn produce other actions. During the transfer of actions it is possible for a discrepancy to occur between the original intention and the actual result. If that happens then, by definition, the author of the algorithm is not in control of, and therefore does not own intellectually from that point on, the resulting process. Theoretically, ownership of an idea is intrinsically connected to the predictability of its outcome, that is, to its intellectual control. Therefore, in the absence of human control the ownership of the algorithmic process must be instead credited to the device that produced it, that is, to the computer. Such a possibility, however, will be objected by those who believe that intellectual ownership can only be credited to an agent that possesses enough intelligence to be aware of its ownership, i.e. possesses consciousness. Unlike humans, computers are not aware of their environment. Perhaps then it may be necessary to define some other kind of awareness that may be only theoretical. This theoretical entity then would be the owner and the reason behind these intellectual phenomena until they possess a physical or legal substance[4].

It is a common belief among architects and designers that the mental process of design is conceived, envisioned, and processed entirely in the human mind and that the computer is merely a tool for organization, productivity, or presentation. Whatever capabilities a computer may have it lacks any level of criticality and its visual effects are nothing but mindless connections to be interpreted by a human designer. It is a common belief that, at best, the computer can serve merely as a processor of information provided as data by the designer and as code by the programmer outputting simply the results of data processed by algorithms. What makes this process problematic is the fact that contrary to common belief algorithms can produce results for which there is no intention or prediction thereof of their behavior. Further, algorithms can also produce algorithms that also are not connected to the intentions or prediction of the original code. This structural behavior resembles in many ways Dadaist poetry, or Markov processes. In those cases, an algorithm functions as a string rewriting system that uses grammar-like rules to operate on strings of symbols in order to generate new strings of text. While the syntax of the resulting text may be consistent with the grammatical rules, the meaning of the resulting text is not necessarily associated semantically with the intentions of the original code. For instance, the introduction of randomness in the arrangement of text can produce results that are unpredictable, but also accidentally meaningful. Unpredictability is, by definition, a disassociation of intention. But unlike chaos, a random rearrangement of elements within a rule-based system produces effects that, although unpredictable, are intrinsically connected through the rules that govern that system. In the field of design, similarities may exist on formal, visual, or structural levels. Computational rearrangement of formal rules that describe, define, and formulate a certain style can produce a permutation of possible formal expressions for that style. For instance, drawing on Andrea Palladio's original designs of villas, Hersey and Freedman[5] were able to detect, extract, and formulate rigorous geometric rules by which Palladio conceived these structures. Using a computational algorithm, they were able to create villa plans and facades that are stylistically indistinguishable from those of Palladio himself. In a similar, almost humorous fashion, the Dadaist engine is a computer algorithm that produces random text based on rearrangement of elements in a grammar. The resulting text, while based on random processes, is readable, often makes sense, and in some cases it is surprisingly intelligent. A version of this algorithm, called the "postmodernism generator," composes essays that appear as if they were developed by a human thinker. While in all of these cases it is quite apparent that awareness, consciousness, or intention is missing, the language patterns produced are convincing enough to lead some to believe that they were authentic, that is, worthy of trust, reliance, or belief, as if they were produced by a sentient author. In one case, a paper constructed using the Dada Engine software was allegedly almost submitted to a conference, which, had it happened, may have passed Turing's classic test of computer intelligence[6].

Unlike grammatical attempts to generate seemingly coherent thoughts based on linguistic patterns encapsulated through sentences, paragraphs, or essays, formalistic languages have already permeated the inspirational, conceptual, and critical aspects of architecture. Computer modeling software is being increasingly used by designers to produce form, shapes, or diagrams that while unaware of their logic are used as a means to address complex problems. Many architects and designers refer to their use of computers as intentional, their language for describing digital practice or formal phenomena has become part of the mainstream nomenclature, and, as a consequence, many so-called digital designs have even been publicized by critics as meaningful. In the last decade, architects have been using the computer as a device to generate, discuss, and critique new forms in an attempt to introduce a new way of thinking about design. While many have attributed the term "tool" to the computer because of its role as a device assisting during the design process, this assumption is not necessarily or entirely true[7]. Computational tools are based on algorithms, that is, processes written by programmers to utilize the arithmetic and logical capabilities of a computer in order to produce certain results. As with mathematicians, the invention or discovery of a mathematical formula does not necessitate the mathematician's knowledge of all the possible uses, repercussions, or consequences of the formula.

Similarly, it is possible that while a programmer has conceived an algorithm that will address a specific problem, the same algorithm might be used to address another completely different problem that was never predicted by the original author. Further, it is possible that using the same algorithm but utilizing different parameters than the ones that were originally designed, may result in a behavior that is completely unexpected. Consequently, when a designer uses an algorithm to design, the designer may not be aware, knowledgeable, or conscious of the mechanisms, specifications, or repercussions of the programmer's algorithm. The gap of discrepancy that separates the programmer from the designer is indeed problematic mainly because of the nature of algorithms. Unlike physical tools where unpredictability is of a mechanical or chemical nature, algorithmic tools are abstract, rational, and intellectual in nature and therefore related to the human mind. So, in that context, the output of an algorithm must be associated to a human mind, either the programmer or the designer. Anything else would be absurd because it would involve an intellectual process without the presence of a human mind. Therefore, critique on the output of an algorithm must be associated to the designer who creatively used the algorithm or to the programmer that made the algorithm available to the designer. In other words, it always has to be a human being responsible for anything that resembles intellectual behavior. However, if someone abandons the humanistic premise and introduces an intellectual entity that, while not identical, nevertheless resembles the human mind, then a different interpretation of design might be possible. Under such a possibility, the human mind is enhanced, complemented, or synergized with an intellectual entity of a computational nature, independent of a human presence, which we will call here otherness, or, in Greek, *allo*. The reason for the existence of such an entity and its disconnection to the human mind is due to the unpredictable, inconceivable, and impossible nature of its origin. In other words, its existence starts where the human mind fails. Consequently, any intelligent behavior by this entity is not a matter of chance, accident, or disguise but rather the output of an allo-logic whose complexity is beyond human comprehension. Armed with such allo-reasoning the human mind can be described as a cyborg, not in the mechanical or electrical sense, but in that of an intellectual one.

While the computer is a device conceived, designed, and built by humans, the processes running within its circuits are not necessarily a human invention as well. Like mathematics or geometry, computation is not an invention but rather a discovery. It is not necessary for a human being to exist in order for computational processes to occur. In other words, computation is of an independent nature and can be implemented on various devices including the computer or, to some extent, the human brain. Otherness is that part of computation that would be described by humans as inconceivable, impossible, unpredictable, or unbelievable, not as linguistic terms but as undiscovered concepts. And yet the possibility that something may exist beyond the comprehensible defines the notion of otherness, that is, of something else. While the human mind has the ability to combine events from the past in order to predict their possibility of existence in the future, otherness is about those possibilities that were missed, overlooked, considered impossible and therefore omitted, or those whose chance of probability were too far into the future or lost into the oblivious past[8]. In any case, their chance to exist is being brought to life by devices that have the ability to perform calculations far more complicated than any human brain or brains together can. However, it is important to mention here that certain tasks or events observed in nature are indeed impossible, yet they are not intellectual. In contrast, impossible tasks related to human thinking are by definition intellectual and, as such, challenge not only the intellectual nature of the human mind but also its own existence.

For the last five decades, beginning with early CAD programs and continuing through high-end computer graphics, modeling, and animation systems, architects have been increasingly concerned with the possible loss of control over their own designs due to the powerful yet complicated, if not mysterious, nature of computers. This concern has led them to position themselves within a wide spectrum of speculations about the effect of computers on design that ranges from complete rejection, elitism, or demonization of their use as design generators to the complete antithesis, that of adoration, worship, or popularization of their use. When comparing avid computer users to those reluctant to engage with them it is necessary to overlook many significant and distinguishing differences in order to identify at least one common theme: the assessment that there is something different, unprecedented, and extraordinary about the computer as it compares to traditional manual tools.

Both non-users and users agree that the effect computers will have on design whether desirable or not will be
significant, profound, and far-reaching. This agreement
is based on an important yet peculiar relationship between
design and its tools. It is apparent that design is strongly
dependent on the tools utilized and, reversely, tools have
a profound effect in design[9]. Traditionally, this dependency
is controlled by the human designers who decide which
tool is to be used when and where as well as the range
of possibilities a tool has for addressing, resolving, or
accomplishing a design task. Further, it is possible that
the use of tools may also have further implications in the
process of addressing a task: just because a tool is available, a task is now possible, or, further, a tool implies
a task. However, a problem arises when the tool is not
entirely under the control of its user. In the case of a
computer as a tool, the results may be unexpected, surprising, or unpredictable even by the users themselves.
While such moments of surprise may be advantageous,
enlightening, or perhaps even undesirable, they do exhibit
a theoretical interest because they challenge the basic
premise of what a tool is or how a tool should behave.
Further, such behavior may lead to alternative ways of
executing the task that were not intended and may lead
to results often superior than intended. Such a possibility
in turn challenges one of design's most existential qualities, that of intention. Is intention necessary in design?
Is intention a human privilege only?

Intention is a term used often in the context of
consciousness. The definition of intention is associated
with a plan on action, a determination to act in a certain
way, a thoughtful and deliberate goal-directedness. In all
cases, intention is attributed (at the absence of any other
source) to the human mind as the source of intention.
Further, intention is also associated with design, because
design is traditionally considered an act of conscious
decision-making with an intention in mind. The problem
with this approach is that it assumes that behind every
decision a conscious mind must be present. However, if
we disassociate the act of decision-making from the
involvement of a conscious plan, if we simply accept that
decisions can be made by unconscious agents, then a
more intricate relationship between decision and intention
emerges than has been previously possible. Rather than
confining the act of deciding within the human domain

a more loose interpretation of decision-making can be established that includes other decision agents not necessarily human. In such a context, the notion of intention does not have to be associated with its source but rather with the process itself. For instance, a design decision may be made by an algorithmic process not intended by the designer, yet as the result of the decision may have been assessed as "successful" the designer may adopt it as one's own idea. In this case, intention was assigned after the fact. While such action is impossible within a humanist world, it is so only in the absence of anything else. Because, if a human is not responsible for an intention then who is?

In response to a possible shift away from the traditional view that the human mind is the central point of reference for any intellectual activity, two theories have been dominant; either a self-referential reconfirmation of the uniqueness of the human mind as the only conscious, sentient, and intelligent system that exists or an acknowledgement that the quantitative limitations of the human mind and the superior computational power of the computer are indications that the human mind is not as central and unique as previously thought. Humanistic approaches to new knowledge have traditionally stressed the importance of self-determination and rejected any dependency on supernatural, mystical, or magical phenomena. In doing so they endorse the ability of humans to rationally determine, evaluate, and justify their actions. Implicit, however, in this determination is the assumption that humans must be in control and therefore be reliable for their thoughts, morality, and actions and not rely on supernatural means. The notion of control is therefore central to the humanistic position. Nonetheless, while the notion of predictability (and consequently responsibility) is typically linked to human control, its negation implies the presence of a supernatural alien realm. Such an alien realm can be unveiled through inductive algorithms since such processes embed an equivocal ability to connect logical patterns with electronic patterns. In the field of design, the notion of unpredictability challenges one of its traditional modes of thought where typically the designer is in full control of the tangible or virtual representation of one's design ideas.

Designers and architects have traditionally maintained control over their design work by employing explanatory, analytical, generative, or representational ideas directly linked to the principles of human understanding and interpretation. Of course, any human-centric approach is associated by definition with subjective phenomena and personal interpretations. Within that realm, any logic that deals with the evaluation or production of form must be, by default, both understandable and open to interpretation and criticism. The problem with this approach is that it does not allow thoughts to transcend beyond the sphere of human understanding. In fact, while it praises and celebrates the uniqueness and complexity of the human mind, it becomes also resistant to theories that point out the potential limitations of the human mind[10].

Intellectual property is defined as the ownership of ideas and control over the tangible or virtual representation of those ideas. Traditionally, designers maintain full intellectual property over their designs or manifestations thereof, based on the assumption that they own and control their ideas. This is not always the case with algorithmic forms. While the hints, clues, or suggestions for an algorithm may be the intellectual property of the designer–programmer, the resulting tangible or virtual representations of those ideas is not necessarily under the control of their author. Algorithms employ randomness, probability, or complexity the outcome of which is unknown, unpredictable, and unimaginable. If there is an intellectual root to these processes it must be sought in a world that extends beyond human understanding[11]. Both the notions of "unknown" and "unimaginable" escape from human understanding since both negate two of the last resorts of human intellect, that of knowledge and imagination. An algorithm is not about perception or interpretation but rather about exploration, codification, and extension of the human mind. Both the algorithmic input and the computer's output are inseparable within a computational system of complementary sources. In this sense, synergy becomes the keyword as an embodiment of a process obtainable through the logic of mutual contributions: that of the human mind and that of the machine's extendibility.

There are often misconceptions about the computer as a machine (i.e. a box with electrical and mechanical interconnections) and its role in the process of design. Design, like many other mental processes, at the information-processing level has nothing specifically "neural" about it.

The functional equivalence between brains and computers does not imply any structural equivalence at an anatomical level (e.g. equivalence of neurons with circuits). Theories of information processes are not equivalent to theories of neural or electronic mechanisms for information processing[12]. Even though, physically, computers may appear to be a set of mindless connections, at the information level they are only a means of channeling mathematical and logical procedures[13]. However, there is indeed a fundamental difference between the quantitative nature of computation and the abstract holistic nature of human thinking.

Is design thought quantifiable? In response to this question, two options appear to be possible; either that design is a process based upon finite elementary units, such as bits, memes, nodes, atoms, etc. or that it is a holistic process with no beginning, end, or any in-between measurable steps. The negation of discreteness implies a continuity of thought that permeates throughout the process of design but is confined within the boundaries of human domain. By definition, subjectivity depends on interpretation and only humans are in a position to do so (yet). Certain intellectual activities, such as intuition, interpretation, choice, or meaning are considered human qualities that can hardly be quantified, if ever. In contrast, the discretization of design opens up a multitude of possibilities as it invites discrete mathematics to be involved in the design process, such as logic, set theory, number theory, combinatorics, graph theory, and probability.

Discretization of design by definition can be addressed, described, and codified using discrete processes executed today by discrete numerical machines (i.e. computers). However, the problem is that discrete/quantitative design provokes a fear of rationalistic determinism that is long considered to be a restraint to the designer's imagination and freedom[14]. Such resistances have attempted to discredit Computer-Aided Design (CAD) products or processes as inadequate, irrelevant, or naïve. According to the humanistic position, design is considered a high-level intellectual endeavor constructed through uniquely human strategies, i.e. intuition, choice, or interpretation. Such theoretical design models negate computation as a possible means for design realization mainly because it is based on discrete processes that are finite and, as such, restrictive.

In contrast, human thought appears to be continuous, infinite, and holistic. However, in practice neither case alone seems adequate enough to serve as a concrete model for design because both suffer from a lack of autonomy. Human designers fail to compute extreme quantitative complexity and computational processes fail to justify consciously even simple decisions. However, these disjunctions result from a logic that seeks to compare two separate, disjointed, and unconnected processes, neither of which has any effect on the other. While traditional human strategies have a long history of success in design, computational strategies are not exclusive, divisive, or restrictive, but rather alien, foreign, different, and, as such, incomparable. Rather than investing in arrested conflicts, both strategies might be better exploited by combining both. What is considered smart in the one world may be considered naïve in the other and vice versa, but by combining both, a common strategy can always be available.

For example, any painting can be represented as a finite grid of finite colors. The exhaustion of all possible combinations of all possible colors within the grid of pixels eventually will reproduce any painting that was ever created in the history of humanity and, as a consequence, any painting yet to be created. Formally, such an argument can be written in the following way:

$$\mathbf{P} = \{(x, y, c)\ x, y, c \in \mathrm{N}, 0 \leq x < w, 0 \leq y < h, 0 \leq c < d\}$$

where $w = 132$, $h = 193$, and $d = 2$. In this case, the possible combinations are $2^{(132 \times 193)} = 10^{7669}$. While the possibility of creating a specific painting, i.e. Matisse's *Icarus*[15], from a random arrangement of colors may appear to be "almost impossible" it is indeed not so; specifically it lies somewhere between 1 and about 10^{7669} possibilities. If there is a possibility, however remote it may be, there must be a chance that it will occur. While the human mind may be bounded to the limitations of quantitative complexity, its computational extension, the computer, allows those boundaries to be surpassed. The notion of "impossible" is no more the assessment of human imagination but rather a degree of probability[16].

In contrast to this example, assessing the notion of possible can be enhanced by another model. This model is based on the idea that, in search of a known target, not all possibilities are equal. Certain possibilities may have a higher chance of success than others. This possibility of possibility opens up a more intricate relationship than has been previously possible. Rather than simply enumerating all possible patterns in search for a known one, genetic algorithms assess each random step. By assessing the degree of promise that a certain pattern has, the notion of selection is introduced in the decision-making process. The selection starts from a population of completely random patterns and occurs in steps (i.e. generations). In each step, the fitness of the whole set of patterns is evaluated, multiple patterns are stochastically selected from the current population (based on their fitness), modified (mutated or recombined) to form a new pattern, which becomes current in the next step of the algorithm. For example, using the previous example, instead of assuming that each random pattern is equal in importance and therefore going through all of them until a perfect match is found, a preferential selection may occur instead. The number of iterations in the case of *Icarus* will be reduced quite significantly from 10^{7669} to merely 3,280,000 (i.e. 3.28×10^6).

Randomness is often associated with lack of control, arbitrariness, and incoherence but more importantly the

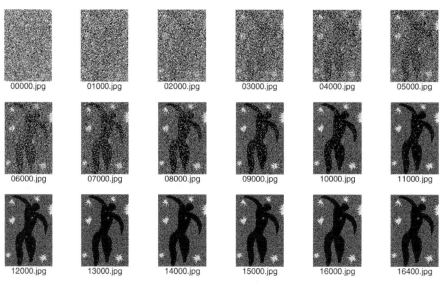

00000.jpg	01000.jpg	02000.jpg	03000.jpg	04000.jpg	05000.jpg
06000.jpg	07000.jpg	08000.jpg	09000.jpg	10000.jpg	11000.jpg
12000.jpg	13000.jpg	14000.jpg	15000.jpg	16000.jpg	16400.jpg

2.1
The phases of a genetic algorithm that seeks to produce an image

possibility of a random occurrence is essentially dependent on time. Possibility is the state occurring within the limits of ability, capacity, or realization in response to both time and resources. So, the question arises as to whether there is anything that cannot be done if one has infinite time and infinite resources? If anything is possible, then isn't merely thinking of something in itself its own definition of being? Information, the root of knowledge, is derived from the prefix *in-* and the noun *formation*. In its linguistic context, information means giving form, figure, shape, and therefore organizational structure to, apparently, formless, figureless, and shapeless notions. Information should be understood not as a passive enumeration of data but rather as an active process of filtering data, not in the trivial sense of awareness, but in the strict sense of logical proof. While the quantity and composition of external data may appear to be infinite, random, or incoherent logical filtering will lead progressively to an ordered formation. Unlike blind randomness, certain algorithms (i.e. genetic) are capable of selectively controlling the shaping of information. Such algorithmic events result from factors that are neither arbitrary nor predictable yet seem to be guided by some sort of intelligence. While these events are made possible by simulating natural processes without involving human intelligence, it is inevitable to assume that some human intelligence is involved in the selection of the natural process that best fits the problem of randomness. Human intelligence arises as an act of preference.

Preference is the grant of favor or advantage to one over another. It is a subjective formation of an idea that leads eventually to choice. As subjective actions are dictated by one's own criteria, a problem arises when such actions refer back to the same person. For instance, an architect, in designing a house for a client, is trained to observe, detect, and address certain preferences of the client. Yet, when the client and the architect are one and the same person, then preferences tend to elude one's own mind. This happens either because one is not able to comprehend fully one's own mind or because one may miss certain aspects. "While one knows what one knows, one certainly does not know what one does not know." This seemingly self-evident statement is not so, in at least two ways. First, the assertion that one is unaware of one's own ignorance is impossible within the sphere of that person's knowledge; for if it were true then one would know what one does not know, which is an apparent contradiction. Second, the fact that the statement is in quotes means that it is being stated by a third person in which case the lack of knowledge of ignorance may be viewed as such from the third person's viewpoint. In other words, only a third person may be able to detect the incompleteness of another person's knowledge.

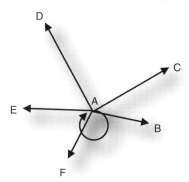

2.2
The relationship between one and another is not the same as with one and itself

In mythology, Ulysses introduced himself to the Cyclops as "nobody." Later on, when the Cyclops was looking for help nobody would help him because *nobody* hurt him. This last statement is self-consistent within its own linguistic context but not if one gets out of the context and assigns the name "nobody" to somebody. Then the whole statement has a different meaning, yet undetected for those inside the system. Godel's incompleteness theorem claims that within any consistent formalization of a quantifiable system a statement can be constructed that can be neither proved nor disproved within that system. The beauty of Godel's argument is not only in pointing out a discrepancy in reasoning but, most importantly, in revealing the existence of an alien realm that bounds the known universe.

Allo can be defined as a representation of something else, not in the sense of a metaphor, but in the realistic sense of referring to something unknown and therefore evasive, whose entrance point, gateway, or portal can be glanced through by negating reason and venturing instead on alternative paths. Allo is by definition a-logical as it

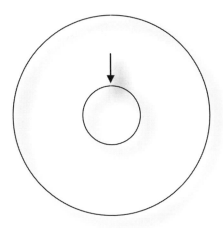

2.3
Observing a system from outside still lies inside another system

arises when the *if-then* clause fails. Yet, while it is not illogical, devoid of logic, or senseless, it represents those
possibilities that are out of the bounds to which the first
logic can apply. Allo is not human; it is a human discovery
that helps describe, explain, and predict lack of knowledge.
It demarcates the end of human reasoning. It is the opposite of "is"; allo is everything else.

Endnotes

[1]Hyperion means "beyond-one" and is also the name of a Titan,
father of Sun, Moon, and Dawn who was considered to be the god
of observation.

[2]Parmenides said: ὡς οὐκ ἐστι μη εἶναι = *what is not, cannot be*
identifying a key separation between "what is" as a logical predicate
and "what is" as a visual interpretation. See Popper, K., *The World
of Parmenides*. London: Routledge, 1998, pp. 70–72.

[3]A set of graphs and tables that describe, assess, and project
the potential of computers appears in the latest book of Ray
Kurzweil. See Kurzweil, R., *The Singularity is Near*. New York: Viking,
2005.

[4]The problem of ownership, jurisdiction, and responsibility of one
human over another is perhaps best documented in the laws of
slavery. If a slave makes a great discovery does it belong to the
master, and vice versa if a slave makes a fatal mistake should the
master be responsible instead?

[5]See Hershey, G. and R. Freedman, *Possible Palladian Villas*: (*Plus a Few Instructively Impossible Ones*). Cambridge: MIT Press, 1992.

[6]The Turing test is a proposal for a test of a machine's capability to perform human-like conversation. Described by Alan Turing in the 1950 paper (Alan Turing, "Computing machinery and intelligence." *Mind*, vol. LIX, no. 236, October 1950, pp. 433–460), it proceeds as follows: a human judge engages in a natural language conversation with two other parties, one a human and the other a machine; if the judge cannot reliably tell which is which, then the machine is said to pass the test. It is assumed that both the human and the machine try to appear human. In order to keep the test setting simple and universal (to explicitly test the linguistic capability of some machine), the conversation is usually limited to a text-only channel such as a teletype machine as Turing suggested.

[7]Architects such as Neil Denari, Greg Lynn, or Peter Eisenman use the term *tool* to describe computational processes yet none of them has any formal education in computer science.

[8]Marcos Novak points out that while the clause "if-then" is a syllogistic structure that leads on to new knowledge, the clause "if-then-else" involves the alternative "else" that may point to the opposite of knowledge, that is, to "that which does not follow from its roots, or, indeed, that whose roots can no longer be traced, or have become irrelevant, or are unknown, or follow from principles outside previous understanding." See Novak. M., "Alien space: the shock of the view," article reproduced from Art + Technology Supplement of CIRCA 90, pp. s12–13.

[9]In the words of Marshall McLuhan "first we build the tools, then they build us." Perhaps, Stanley Kubrick and Arthur Clarke's movie "2001: Space Odyssey" is a good fictional example of this possibility.

[10]Strange as it may sound, acknowledging lack of control is, in a way, more human than rejecting it. Humanism is not about rejecting anything that threatens human control but rather about accepting limitations and working towards solutions.

[11]Sir Karl Popper argued that the world as a whole consists of three interconnected worlds. World One, is the world of physical objects and their properties – with their energies, forces, and motions. World Two is the subjective world of states of consciousness, or of mental states – with intentions, feelings, thoughts, dreams, memories, and so on, in individual minds. World Three is the world of objective contents of thought, especially of scientific and poetic thoughts and of works of art. World Three is a human product, a human creation, which creates in its turn theoretical

systems with their own domains of autonomy. See Popper, K. R., *The Logic of Scientific Discovery*. New York: Harper & Row, 1968.

[12]The works of Herbert Simon and Allen Newel in the 1960s and 1970s are undoubtedly some of the best examples of the study of artificial intelligence.

[13]Greg Lynn, in *Animate Form*. New York: Princeton Architectural Press, 1999, p. 19, describes machine intelligence "as that of mindless connections."

[14]Colin Rowe's criticism on Alexander's *Notes on the Synthesis of Form* and consequently extending it to all value-free empirical facts is that they are only "attempts to avoid any imputation of prejudice." See p. 78 in Rowe, C. and F. Koetter, "Collage city", in *Architectural Review 158*, no. 942, August 1975, pp. 66–90.

[15]Icarus, the son of Daedalus (creator of the Labyrinth), is a metaphor for an impossible task, consequent failure, yet eternal remembrance. Of course, any bitmap image of those dimensions would require the same number of calculations.

[16]A single processor working 1000 GIPS can only perform 10^{18} operations in a year. So, if 10^{400} computers will work in parallel (because the problem is not sequential), they will be finished in a year; or 10^{800} computers in half a year. In other words, 10^{7K} is indeed an impossible number for us but not necessarily so for a network of computers.

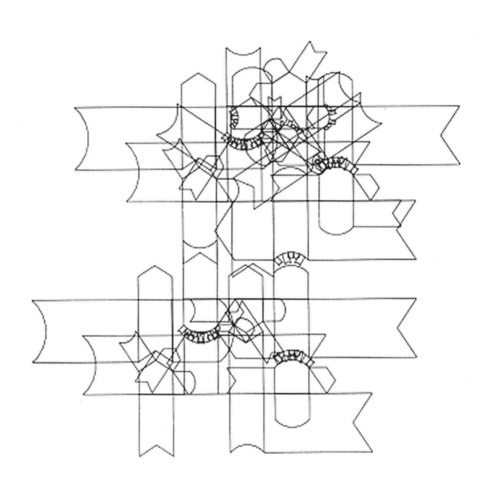

3 A brief history of algotecture

Algotecture is a term coined here to denote the use of algorithms in architecture. This term differs from the popular terms *CAD* or *computer graphics* in the sense that algorithms are not necessarily dependent on computers whereas the former are, at least, by definition. This distinction is very important as it liberates, excludes, and disassociates the mathematical and logical processes used for addressing a problem from the machine that facilitates the implementation of those processes. Such a use involves the articulation of a strategy for solving problems whose target is known, as well as to address problems whose target cannot be defined. Within the realm of computer graphics, solutions can be built for almost any problem whose complexity, amount, or type of work justifies the use of a computer. For instance, in architectural practice, inputting data points, calculating structural elements, or printing large line drawings are tasks, or problems, that require the use of the computer even though they can be performed manually. Yet, there are some problems whose complexity, level of uncertainty, ambiguity, or range of possible solutions required a synergetic relationship between the human mind and a computer system. Such a synergy is possible only through the use of algorithmic strategies that ensure a complementary and dialectic relationship between the human mind and the machine.

In the world of design, and in particular architecture, the problems designers are called upon to solve are not necessarily solvable in the traditional sense of finding a path between A and B. Apart from specific quantitative localized subproblems that occur within some standardized patterns of construction, the general formal, aesthetic, or planning considerations are barely addressable as discrete solvable problems. Consequently, it may be more appropriate to use the term *problem-addressing* rather than *problem-solving*. Whatever the choice is, an algorithm serves as a means for articulating the problem whether solvable or addressable. More importantly, because of its translational power, an algorithm can carry out that articulation one step further and process it using a computer's arithmetic and logical power. The combination of both systems, that is, that of the human and that of the computer, is where the true power of algorithms lies. An algorithm is not a game, a cool name, another tool, or an obscure engineers' conspiracy but instead it is a way of thinking, and because of its newly introduced counterpart, the computer, it allows human thoughts to extend beyond their limitations. Because design is a way of thinking intrinsically weaved with the most existential human characteristics, that of logic, artificiality, creativity, and identity, algorithms serve as the means to explore beyond, in parallel, or in lieu of traditional established ways of thinking. The notion of addressability versus solvability is important in design because it allows the algorithms to address a problem offering hints, suggestions, or alternatives which may never have occurred to the human designer. In such a synergetic relationship the unpredictable, impossible, or unknown are not factors of fear but rather invitations for exploration.

In design, algorithms can be used to solve, organize, or explore problems with increased visual or organizational complexity. In its simplest form, a computational algorithm uses numerical methods to address problems. Numbers are often regarded as discrete quantitative units that are utilized for measuring, yet in computational terms numbers can be constructed that can address an infinite degree of division thus exhibiting theoretical continuity. The basic linguistic elements used in algorithms are constants, variables, procedures, classes, and libraries and the basic operations are arithmetical, logical, combinatorial, relational, and classificatory arranged under specific grammatical and syntactical rules. These elements and operations are designed to address the numerical nature of computers while at the same time provide the means for composing logical patterns. For example, pixels on a computer screen are numerical elements defined by their color value and their x and y coordinates, but at the same time they can be addressed as visual compositions defined by logical patterns.

Historically, algorithms have been used quite extensively in architecture. While the connotation of an algorithm may be associated with computer science, nonetheless the use of instructions, commands, or rules in architectural practice are, in essence, algorithms. The rationalization of the design process in an architectural practice involves by necessity the use of structured, discrete, and well-defined instructions for the accomplishment of design projects and the distribution of labor among the designers of a project. Implicitly within the concept of a design algorithm is perhaps the assumption of a lack of formal or aesthetic sensitivity due to the rational and technocratic connotations associated with mathematical and logical processes. The dominant mode for using computers in architecture today is a combination of manually driven design decisions and formally responsive computer applications. The problem with this combination is that neither the designer is aware of the possibilities that computational schemes can produce nor the software packages are able to predict the moves, idiosyncrasies, or personality of every designer. Therefore, the result is a distancing between the potential design explorations and the capacity built into computational tools. Designers often miss the opportunity opened up to them through digital tools, merely because of lack of understanding that computation can be part of the design process as well.

While some digital designers are claiming to be great fans, users, or explorers of digital design, a lack of knowledge on what really constitutes digital design contributes towards a general misunderstanding; the use of computer applications is not per se an act of digital design. Digital, in the true sense of the meaning, is about the reduction of a process into discrete patterns and the articulation of these patterns into new entities to be used by a computer. Digital is an achievement of the collective organizational properties of computers not the intrinsic nature of the appearance of their products. In other words, digital is a process not a product. If it is seen as a process, then the emphasis is placed on understanding, distinguishing, and discerning the means by which design can enter the world of computation, and not the other way around. The world of computational design is quite different from the manual world of design. Terms, concepts, and processes that are seen as inconceivable, unpredictable, or simply impossible by a human designer can be explored, implemented, and developed into entirely new design strategies within the digital world. Instead, what is happening is the use of computers as marketing tools of strange forms whose origin, process, or rationale of generation is entirely unknown and so they are judged on the basis of their appearance often utilizing mystic, cryptic, or obfuscating texts for explanation.

In the last two decades, architecture has transformed from a manually driven tool-based design and practice profession to a computer-driven form-based design and global practice. This transformation, while impressive, has not yet reached its full potential. Partially because of the lack of computational education of architects or the plethora of confusing literature on digital design, there is hardly any bright examples of using computers in their full potential as design tools. Corporate architectural practices, such as SOM, NBBJ, or RTKL, use the computer simply as an efficiency tool while continuing to develop design through traditional manual means, and prominent avant-garde practices, such as Gehry, Morphosis, or Zaha Hadid, use the computer as a means of marketing and presentation, despite their unsubstantiated claims to the opposite. Occasionally, there are some young architects fresh out of school who may be able to use computational methods in design. Yet the majority of architecture practices, despite their appearance, are still developing ideas through their own human minds or by simplistic NURBS-based formal mongering.

Design, as defined by a few prominent theorists, is about virtuality, not actuality[1]. In its conception it is about something vague, indefinite, and uncertain, not necessarily the sudden appearance of a form (for that would be certain) but rather about a combination of thoughts that lead to the inception of a form. Algorithmic logic is about the articulation of thoughts and a vague struggle to explore possibilities of existential emergence. When composing an algorithm one is dealing with a symbolic language whose vocabulary, syntax, and meaning is closely dependent on the features of a digital computer. In contrast to a physical language which is dependent on its communicative power between human beings, algorithms are based on a language which is dependent on its communicative power between a human and a computer. Such a dependency is not superior, inferior, or equivalent but rather complementary. On communicating a task to a human being one is forced to take under consideration the limitations or capabilities of a human being which are known, pre-estimated, and predictable. However, on communicating a task to a computer one should not assume the same capabilities or limitations of a human being. The computer is not a human mind. It is not a human designer. It is rather a counterpart to human imagination, a source of ideas, and a portal into another world new to the human mind.

The problem with algorithmic logic in design is that fixed interrelationships between numbers and concepts appear to some designers as too deterministic. In fact, many designers are not interested in the mathematics of a design composition but rather in the composition itself. While this position may be interpreted as a defense mechanism against the possible rationalization of design, it becomes also an obstacle in exploring the limits of a possible rationalization of design. Computer systems that are referred to as CAD systems are in essence collections of algorithms each of which addresses a specific graphical design issue. A user of a CAD system, i.e. a designer, makes use of these algorithms without knowledge of how they work and consequently is unable to determine the full value of their potential. While CAD systems helped designers significantly to organize, speed up, or communicate ideas using high-level commands, only a few CAD systems offer the means to combine those commands algorithmically in ways that would allow one to explore "out of the box" possibilities or to break down the commands in ways that would allow one to explore what is "under the hood." Further, very few designers have the knowledge to understand the computational mechanisms involved in a CAD system, or, reversely, very few CAD developers are also equally accomplished designers.

Architectural design has a long history of addressing complex programmatic requirements without a specific design target. Unlike other design fields where the target is to solve a particular problem in the best possible way, architectural design is open-ended, in flux, and uncertain. Codified information, such as standards, codes, specifications, or types, simply serve the purpose of conforming to functional requirements, yet are not guarantees for a successful design solution. Deciding under uncertainty requires experience, intuition, and ingenuity. Ingenuity is an inventive skill of imagination, creativity, and resourcefulness, and should not be confused with imitation, problem solving, or planning.

To identify the problem of design in general, and of architectural design in particular, it is necessary to describe and understand the *process* of design. While many definitions and models of design exist, most agree that "design is a process of inventing physical things which display new physical order, organization, form, in response to function."[2] However, since no formula or predetermined steps exist which can translate form and function into a new, internally consistent physical entity, design has been held to be an art rather than a science. It is considered to be an iterative, "trial-and-error" process that relies heavily on knowledge, experience, and intuition.

Traditionally, intuition is a basis of many design theories, often referred to as "black box" theories. According to them, design, as well as its evaluation, tends to be highly subjective. While such a position relieves the designers from explaining, justifying, or rationalizing their decisions and actions, it also enables the designer and a circle of critics to exercise authoritative power. The problem with this is not necessarily in the lack of objective criteria but rather in the lack of rational consistency. If design is to be studied as a process, then a series of reasonable, justifiable, and consistent steps should be established. The presence of intuition as a source of inspiration, decision, or action is considered arbitrary, obscure, and, as such, "black."

In contrast, another set of theories defines the design process as a *problem-solving process*. According to the latter, design can be conceived as a systematic, finite, and rational activity. As defined by researchers over the past 40 years, for every problem a solution space exists, that is, a domain that includes all the possible solutions to a problem. Problem-solving then can be characterized as a process of searching through alternative solutions in this space to discover one or several which meet certain goals and may, therefore, be considered *solution states*. Alternatively, a problem space does not always necessitate the identification of a solution as a target, but instead may involve simply addressing the problem for possible alternative solutions that are not known in advance. In many cases, the solution to a design problem may deviate from the original objectives. For instance, a Markov process is a finite state algorithm with probabilities for each transition so that a next state is found given that the current state is known. In that way, a design problem may be addressed not only in a deterministic but also in a probabilistic manner.

In the early 1960s, a need for rationality in the design process was beginning to gain ground, due primarily to the rise of the computer, as an arithmetic and logical device. If design is a conceptual interaction between the context's demands and the adjustments of the form, then there may be a way to encode it as a process by making an abstract picture of the problem, which will retain only its abstract structural features, i.e. an algorithm. By introducing set theory, structural analysis, and the theory of computation as tools for addressing the design problem, quantitative elements or events associated with the design problem could be represented by Boolean variables, that is, logical binary variables[3] and later by fuzzy logic, that is, partial truth variables. This approach was followed by a flurry of related research into the field of design. But the rationalization of design was much more far-reaching. It introduced computers into the design process by suggesting which aspects of the design process are amenable to systematization and which are not. While some steps during the design process are based on rational decisions, some are not. This suggests that the design process is open-ended and that it entails frequent changes of mind or changes of constraints and that a computer-based design system should permit them to occur.

However, because of the large number of constraints to be simultaneously considered in an architectural design problem, it would be difficult to meet them all. The complexity of the design problem is so great that a designer would be unable to arrive at an appropriate solution unless a new way could be found to break down the problem into subproblems and use a non-deterministic approach to solve them. While hierarchical approaches are key factors in addressing extreme complexity, they are also prone to loss of the holistic picture of a design problem, where perhaps the whole is not simply the sum of its parts. For instance, one of the areas where the

computer was helpful to an architect is in space allocation, that is, in resolving the programmatic requirements
of a building (spaces, footage, orientation and neighbor-
ing conditions) and arranging the spaces under the
requirements' constraints. However, while the resulting
space allocation schemes were indeed correct, or at
least optimally placed, the overall schemes lacked certain organizational, aesthetic, or identifiable characteristics. Yet, many of these systems are still used in
engineering design where the objective is to optimize an
overly complicated design without any aesthetic concerns. In architecture these systems are used in a sug-
gestive manner, that is, at a sufficiently early stage of the
design process where a large number of possible
schemes are sought and the best ones are chosen for
further development.

Another approach to addressing architectural design as
a problem-solving process is that of *structural linguistics*.
Here, the designer attempts to structure the problem

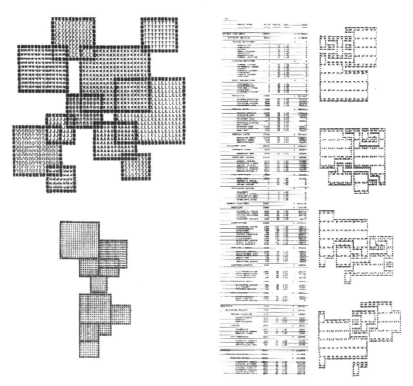

3.1
Output of a space allocation program

by grouping the constraints into thematic areas (e.g. zoning, circulation, structure), and proceeding to design by considering each group of constraints more or less independently. This information is converted into linguistic structures through the use of transformational rules. Then, the designer represents these linguistic structures in the form of sentences[4], that is, specific sets of architectural elements which include not only the elements but also the rules which allow a designer to combine them into feasible and meaningful architectural compositions. The aim of this approach became one of writing algorithms for the generation of feasible and meaningful architectural "sentences." Structural linguistic algorithms have been written for the design of buildings, or rather, for designing parts of buildings. Over half of these algorithms have been concerned with *space allocation* problems, some of which resulted in formal definitions or languages which the computer can be programmed to resolve[5].

Some theorists have argued that many problems cannot be solved algorithmically[6], either because the procedure leading to their solution is ill-defined or because not all the information needed to solve them is available or accurate. Such problems make it necessary to use *heuristic and adaptive decision procedures*. Heuristic methods typically rely on trial-and-error techniques to arrive at a solution. Such techniques are, by definition, much closer to the *search-and-evaluate* processes used in architectural design. In adaptive procedures, the computer itself learns by experience[7], that is, by creating a database of information based on external observation of the designer's decisions. This approach became the basis system, known as *expert systems*. Here knowledge about a specific area of human expertise is codified as a set of rules. By means of dialogue with the user, the system arrives at a solution to a particular problem. New knowledge is provided by the user to the knowledge base without a programmer having to rewrite or reconfigure the system. The ability of the system to justify conclusions and to explain reasoning leads to further systematization of the design process, but also, sometimes, to paradoxes in the computer's reasoning.

Because of its quantitative nature, the study of complexity involves by necessity computational methods as means of analysis, simulation, and synthesis of systems that involve large amounts of information or information processing. Unlike traditional methods of analysis and synthesis, computational schemes offer a degree of rationality that allows them to migrate into computer-executable programs. Such a possibility opens up enormous potential than has been previously possible; rather than utilizing mere human-based intelligence in resolving design problems, a complementary synergetic relationship between humans and computers becomes possible. Ideally, in such a framework, both parties can contribute each one's unique strengths in an attempt to seek, explore, invent, or discover principles and methods of design. Computing becomes the essential link between the two systems.

As a result of growing computer capabilities, the rationalization of design engendered a great number of expectations. Unfortunately, most of these expectations were not met, perhaps because machine intelligence was overestimated. Architectural design is a much more complicated process than many other design processes because it entails factors that cannot be codified or predicted. The heuristic processes that guide the search rely not only on information pertinent to the particular problem, but also on information which is indirectly related to it and inferred by the context. In addition, all the information that pertains to the design process does not exist from the beginning. Therefore, many decisions are made during the design process based on information that emerges later that is often impossible to predict.

These problems, as well as the practical needs of architectural offices, led to changes in the approach. Rather than competing with, emulating, or replacing designers, the approach in the 1970s was predicated on the belief that they should assist, complement or augment the design process. The machine was introduced as an aid to instruction, as a mediator for the goals and aspirations of the architects. The computer could communicate with architects by accepting information, manipulating it, and providing useful output. In addition to synthesizing form, computers are also able to accept and process non-geometric information about form. Therefore, it is necessary for architectural design languages to be invented to describe operations on building databases. One pioneering effort in this area is GLIDE, a language which allowed the user to assemble buildings[8]. Another approach in the direction of computer-augmented architectural design was the manipulation of architectural forms according to rules[9]. Basic structural and functional elements were assembled to make volumes (elements of composition) which, in turn, were assembled to make buildings. All elements were stored in the computer's memory in symbolic form, and the user operated on them by manipulating symbols in accordance with rules derived through the classic academic tradition.

As design began to be increasingly thought of as a systematic and rational activity, many of its empirical and experimental rules were explored. By operating on symbolic structures stored in the computer's memory and manipulating them according to rules, computers could reason about, or even predict, the behavior of a simulated environment. The machines were made to carry out a "make-believe" happening, a *simulation*. Numerous simulation models were formulated and much progress was made toward simulating design states[10]. These models simulated the states of a designed environment and the transitions from one state to another. Yet, no model was formulated which could encompass both the relationships between the components of a building and its environment. Even though simulation models are valuable tools for predicting and evaluating performance, their contribution to the architectural design process has been marginal. They leave the interpretation of the symbols they represent and the relationships between them to the designer. The transition from one design state to the next must be done by the designer with little or no assistance by the computer.

Augmented design failed to improve the architectural design process and products. The majority of the systems that have been installed worldwide are used for drafting or site planning, which are not, in themselves, essential steps in the process of architectural design[11]. Perhaps the reluctance of CAD research to improve the architectural design process and products is probably due to the fact that most of the researchers did not consider the idiosyncrasies of architectural design. In architecture, design quality is reflected in forms and their relationships. Many architects and theorists have argued that what distinguishes a well-designed building from one that is poorly designed can only be found in the morphological relations that the former embodies. "One can have a beautiful idea of winning a chess game. One can brutally win a chess game in a very inelegant way. But there can be an elegance in the process of winning itself, that is poetic."[12]

Form-based design is viewed as an activity, which entails invention and exploration of new forms and their relations. Various methods of analysis have been employed in the search for new forms: formal analysis involves the investigation of the properties of an architectural subject. Compositional principles, geometrical attributes, and morphological properties are extracted from figural appearances of an object. In contrast, structural analysis deals with the derivation of the motivations and propensities which are implicit within form and which may be used to distinguish the difference between what is and what appears to be.

One approach to form-based design is that of *shape grammars*[13]. They were developed to carry out spatial computations visually and are used to generate designs based on production rules. A shape grammar consists of rules and an initial shape. There are two types of shape grammars. In standard grammars, each rule is defined explicitly by a pair of shapes separated by an arrow. The shape on the left side of the arrow determines the part of the shape to which the rule is to be applied. The shape on the right side of the arrow determines the shape that results when the rule is employed. In this context, shape grammars contribute rationality, consistency, and traceability where finite production rules are applied. Shape grammars can be associated with linguistic patterns and therefore illustrate meaningful statements that may in turn produce languages of design. However, as shape grammars are based on a clearly defined set of rules leaving no place for ambiguity, they have been used extensively for the generation of patterns, diagrams, and floor layouts.

An interesting variation of shape grammars is that of *fractal generative systems*. Based on a scheme, formulated by the German mathematician Von Koch, a fractal process consists of an initial shape (the base) and one or more generators. From a practical point of view, the generator is a production rule: each and every line segment of the base is replaced by the shape of the generator. The implementation of an interactive computer program has been reported by Yessios which allows the fractal to be generated one at a time or at multiple increments, backwards or forwards. As described by Yessios, "a building typically has to respond to a multiplicity of processes, superimposed or interwoven. Therefore, the fractal process has to be guided, to be constrained and to be filtered. The fractal process has to be 'mutated' by the utilitarian requirements of the functionalities of a building."[14]

Another approach to formalistic design is that of *morphing*. It involves two important principles of architectural form: stability and change. Morphing is not exactly a form-making

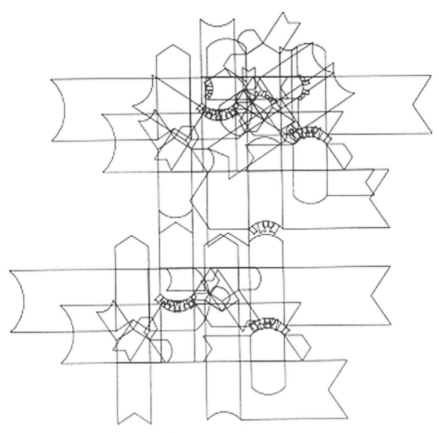

3.2
Studies on fractal processes for the Frankfurt Biocentrum by C. Yessios and P. Eisenman

procedure because the subject of transformation must already be complete. During a transformation, only relations change. No new elements can be introduced or removed; nothing is added or subtracted from the scene. However, the illusion of movement, often described as "frozen music," has been argued to have a high architectonic value[15]. It illustrates the forces designers have referred to, as "punctured volumes," "compressed planes," "interpenetrating spaces," or "agitated surfaces." One pioneering exploration of *morphing in architecture* has been reported by Terzidis[16]. According to him an initial shape A can be transformed to a target shape B by applying any number of in-between steps. All the points of shape A are mapped onto shape B and vice versa. Furthermore, once the rules of transition have been established, the transition can be allowed to continue extrapolating beyond its target.

In contrast to automated or augmented design, form-based design has the advantage of allowing one to delve into the idiosyncrasies of architectural form. Its disadvantage is that it is perceived as being too iconolatric, superficial, and conformist[17]. As a consequence, form-based design has been regarded suspiciously as combining the icons of historical architecture and technological development at a surface level.

Because of its uncertain, indefinite, and ambivalent nature there is hardly a single or unified definition of design. The problem with this, however, is that because words are just shells into which notions are packed, the misuse of language may alter one's genuine relation to notions[18]. In fact, it appears that the terms *design* and *planning* are often used interchangeably as one and the same thing. While in the world of arts and architecture design is associated with human creativity, ingenuity, and intuition, in the world of engineering a more rational, confined, organized, and methodical model exists. It suggests functionality, performance, and conformity, while, at the same time, it may be resistant to emotion, humor, allegory, metaphor, or analogy. As the world of science seeks, within diverse disciplines, to find a set of principles that govern the field of design, a need arises to integrate two seemingly contrasting worlds, that of science and that of the arts.

What makes design problematic for scientists and engineers is that they have maintained a doctrine of *rationalistic determinism* in their fields. It is the theory that the exercise of reason provides the only valid basis for action or belief and that reason is the prime source of knowledge. Because of its clarity and efficiency, rationalistic determinism has traditionally been a dominant mode of thought in the world of science. The problem with this is that it assumes that all human activities abide to the same principles. In contrast, design, as defined in the arts and architecture, is based on quite different, if not opposite, principles. Rather than following a rationalistic model, designers often employ the acceptance of empiricism, authority, spiritual revelation, metaphor or analogy as sources for their design inspiration. In addition, they quite often defy the rules of scientific planning and scheduling. This mode of thought, which we call here *intuition*, comes in contrast to the dominant model of science where rational, methodical, and systematic processes exist. More than ever now, as design enters the world of science, or as science enters the world of design, a complementing and harmonious mix of both thought processes is needed.

In some design practices, rational and intuitive approaches to design have been incorporated quite successfully within the same business structure. For instance, *architectural practice* is a business model where intuitive design is a significant part. Here intuition is separated from the production phase where sketching, brainstorming, iterative drawings, visual analogies, and metaphorical notions are utilized. The project management and scheduling at that stage consists only of mere deadlines rather than processes or methods. Once a design idea is agreed upon, the architects move into the production phases where most business models and methods are applicable. What makes architectural practice most exceptional is that it is the same people that are involved in both intuitive and rational activities. In contrast, in other creative business practices, such as, for instance, the movie industry, different people are involved in different activities each of which is an expert within one's own domain. Therefore integration of different talents and expertise becomes a major business management challenge.

For the last three decades, beginning with Christopher Alexander's *Notes of the Synthesis of Form* and Robert Venturi's *Complexity and Contradiction in Architecture* and continuing through a plethora of formal studies and computational methods[19], designers, architects and urban planners have been primarily concerned with increased complexity involved in the design of buildings, urban areas, and cities. Research and professional practice have attempted to automate traditional "manual" methods of production using computer-aided design tools and to consider architectural schools and offices as hubs for crosspollination between diverse engineering disciplines. When comparing architectural design and other software-intensive engineering design disciplines it is necessary to overlook many significant and distinguishing differences in order to identify at least one common theme: the use of computational methods to address excessively complex tasks.

Complexity is a term used to denote the length of a description of a system or the amount of time required to create a system. From networks and computers to machines and buildings there is a great deal of effort spent on how to understand, explain, model, or design systems whose scope, scale, and complexity often challenge the ability of designers to fully comprehend them. While complexity may be a characteristic of many natural systems or processes, within the field of design the study of complexity is associated with artificial, synthetic, and human-made systems. Such systems, despite being human creations, consist of parts and relationships arranged in such complicated ways that often surpass a single designer's ability to thoroughly comprehend them even if that person is their own creator. Paradoxical as it may appear, humans today have become capable of exceeding their own intellect. Through the use of intricate algorithms, complex computations, and advanced computer systems designers are able to extend their thoughts into a once unknown and unimaginable world of complexity. Yet, the inability of the human mind to single-handedly grasp, explain, or predict artificial complexity is caused mainly by quantitative constraints, that is, by the *amount* of information or the *time* it takes to compute it and not necessarily to the intellectual ability of humans to learn, infer, or reason about such complexities.

Both architects and engineers argue for the deployment of computational strategies for addressing, resolving, and satisfying complicated design requirements. These strategies result from a logic, which is based on the premise that systematic, methodical, and rational patterns of thought are capable of resolving almost any design problem. While this assumption may be true for well-defined problems, most design problems are not always clearly defined. In fact, the notion of design as an abstract, ambiguous, indefinite, and unpredictable intellectual phenomenon is quite attuned to the very nature of the definition or perhaps lack of a single definition of design. Yet, the mere existence of certain ambiguous qualities such as amphiboly, indefiniteness, vagueness, equivocation, ambivalence, or coexistence serve as patterns, metaphors, and encapsulations that facilitate in detecting, understanding, and addressing complex notions. The most paradigmatic example of this practice is the case of architect Frank Gehry. In his office, design solutions are not sought through methodical computer-aided design methods but rather by the use of encapsulated symbolic schemes, such as metaphors, allegories, or analogies. The design teams spend countless hours of thought, modeling, iterative adjustment, and redesign based on the metaphor of a crinkled piece of paper or an ambiguous napkin sketch. Complexity emerges not as a sum of the parts but rather as a reference to a model that serves the purpose of a metaphor. Rather than using direct, explicit, or unequivocal terms to communicate, designers often use instead ambiguous, tacit, or metaphorical means. For instance, designers often use non-verbal means of communication such as sketches, drawings, analogies, expressions, gestures, or metaphors. What makes verbal communication so problematic for creative people is that it is too literal, leaving little, if any, ground for interpretation. It assumes that for every notion or idea there is a word or a phrase to describe it, but that may not be the case for those *yet to be defined* design concepts. In contrast, implicit and tacit information suggests much more than their spoken counterparts.

Any scientific approach to design needs to take into consideration, not only systematic, methodical, and rational models, but also alternative approaches that address the nature of design as an indefinite, ill-defined, and intuitive process. The ultimate goal of a design project is the development of an innovative frame breaking solution or process. Innovation involves originality and originality involves departure from previous practices. Design is about the fresh, new, unusual, and inventive. More often than not, design projects stand out not only because they satisfy the requirements but mainly because they are imaginative, unexpected, and ingenious.

While the original goal of CAD was to free the designer from repetitive, tedious, or time-consuming tasks, it also sought to empower the designer with the means to explore beyond the traditional framework of manual design. The desire to implicate a digital mode of thought within the design process was intimately linked to the nature of computation and its close association with that of design. If design is to be considered a systematic, finite, and rational activity then a computational scheme could be devised that would encapsulate, codify, and reflect the process. Further, such a scheme could be transferred and processed using a computational device such as a computer. The initial thought was that because computation employs complex processes, such as simulation, optimization, permutation, or transformation, such processes could be applicable, useful, if not catalytic in addressing design problems. However, due to the complex nature of the processes, very few designers were in a position to understand and implement them in a meaningful way in design.

As most of the researchers in CAD were primarily concerned with the technicalities of converting design ideas into digital tools, none, if any, was also concerned with using those tools to actually design. Apparently, the design sensitivities involved in creating a tool are not the same as those involved with using one. The unprecedented potentiality of the new CAD tools brought a high expectation of how to change the way designers work, create, and think. Therefore, a paradigm shift was sought from within the designer's world, one that would occur by employing the newly created CAD tools. However, it may be argued here that the long awaited paradigm shift occurred not in the designer's mind but in the programmer's mind. It is the programmer that invented the tool and set out the workspace, capabilities, and limitations for the designer to work within. CAD software developers are meta-designers, i.e. designers of design-systems. In contrast, the traditional designers-turned-digital are merely spectators to a world that extends beyond their comprehension. For the last two decades, beginning with Eisenman's visions and

Lynn's curvilinearity and continuing through an over-whelming plethora of so-called digital design studies, architects have been primarily concerned with the formal manifestation of scientific theories using the computer as a medium of expression. Instead of using computational theories as the structural foundation for architectural experimentation, they employed humanistic philosophical theories of the 60s and 70s to explain the complexity of the forms they produced using computers. These practices have attempted to seek for a theoretical foundation of digital phenomena within the scope of classic humanistic methods, i.e. observation, explanation, or interpretation. While such methods are among the fundamental sources of knowledge, they cannot explain the realm of computational phenomena because these extend beyond the sphere of human understanding. Concepts such as randomness, infinity, limit, infinitesimal, or even more elaborate concepts such as complexity, emergence, or recursion are incomprehensible by the human mind not because they are metaphysical, magical, or mysterious but rather because they depend on intellectual means that are external and foreign to the human mind. Instinctively, in the absence of anything else, humans throughout their history have always tried to overcome their material nature by seeking concepts and ideas that are out or independent from their own existence. Perhaps for the first time, through the invention of the computer, a device originally intended to serve people, ironically they were faced with phenomena that demarcated the limits of the human mind and cast some light into the corners of an alien world.

While humanistic approaches praise and celebrate the uniqueness and complexity of the human mind they also become resistant to theories that point out its potential limitations. Late modernist, phenomenological, or cultural critical theories differ significantly from those of mathematics, linguistics, or computation in that the former use as reference the human consciousness whereas the latter seek to separate the subject from the object, seeking instead principles that lay out or are independent of human existence. The use of human presence as a witness of phenomena is a strong underlying framework upon which humanistic theories are based. In contrast, scientific theories tend to quantify events objectifying their effect in order to avoid human interpretation. In the architectural theories of the past 20 years, a certain predominant group of theoreticians, following the traces of humanistic philosophies, have been seeking to find origins, sources, or connections between humanism and digital phenomena. This approach is understandable and expected especially by a group of people that have a deep understanding of humanistic philosophies. The problem, however, with this approach is that it doesn't take under consideration alternative theories, concepts, or methods that are perhaps alien, foreign, and even antithetical to the dominant traditional humanistic philosophies.

Most computational theories become incomprehensible, unintelligible, or incomplete if they are not understood as part of a complementary interaction between the mind and the computer. Because of the external nature of computation, mere reading, studying, or speculating on its theoretical implications is not sufficient enough to grasp its hidden mechanisms. In contrast, actual implementation (i.e. programming) reveals mechanisms, events, or phenomena that defy human explanation. In architecture, this dichotomy was expressed by two antithetical thought camps, formulated by two dialectically opposed ideologies: that of tool-makers and that of tool-users. The first ideology, rooted in the principles of computation, strived to offer the means for design explorations using computers as vehicles. The main protagonists of this ideological camp are software developers, computer scientists, and mathematicians. In contrast, the second ideology sought to connect humanistic philosophies with digital phenomena. In doing so it had to search for ideas or principles within the humanities that may explain or address digital phenomena. For instance, Lynn argues that the plasticity of computer generated forms may be associated with Deleuze's descriptions of smoothness and continuity, as if software is associated with softness. While this may hold some value at a phenomenal level, it certainly holds no truth at a mathematical level. Polynomial-based curves or surfaces, i.e. NURBS, exhibit a continuous and smooth behavior only when implemented on a computer system. It is the numerical representation, processing power, and display resolution of a computer system that makes the plasticity possible, something unknown and perhaps irrelevant to Deleuze[20]. However, concepts such as numerical processing or resolution are not human and therefore cannot be credited. Instead, in the absence of a sentient identifiable human creator, a philosopher's position seems more appropriate. In such a way, humanism is credited, praised, and celebrated by its fellow supporters in a self-referential manner. This anthropocentric attitude is even clearer in Lynn's comparison of a computer with a pet[21]. The use of the words *domesticate* and *wilderness* are characteristic of an anthropocentric and human-dominating attitude rather than a synergistic and collaborative one.

What makes algorithmic logic so problematic for architects is that they have maintained an ethos of artistic sensibility and intuitive playfulness in their practice. In contrast, because of its mechanistic nature, an algorithm is perceived as a non-human creation and therefore is considered distant and remote. Traditionally, the dominant mode for discussing creativity in architecture has always been that of intuition and talent, where stylistic ideas are pervaded by an individual, a "star," or a group of talented partners within the practice. In contrast, an algorithm is a procedure, the result of which is not necessarily credited to its creator. Algorithms are understood as abstract and universal mathematical operations that can be applied to almost any kind or any quantity of elements. For instance, an algorithm in computational geometry is not about the person who invented it but rather about its efficiency, speed, and generality. Consequently, the use of algorithms to address formal problems is regarded suspiciously by some[22] as an attempt to overlook human identity and creativity and give credit instead to an anonymous, mechanistic, and automated procedure[23]. In any case, algorithms are encapsulations of processes or systems of processes that allow one to leap and adventure into the world of the unknown whether natural or artificial. They are not the end product, but rather a vehicle for exploration. What distinguishes these processes from common "problem-solving" is that their behavior is often non-predictable and that frequently they produce patterns of thought and results that amaze even their own creators.

Computation is a term that differs from, but is often confused with, computerization. While computation is the procedure of calculating, i.e. determining something by mathematical or logical methods, computerization is the act of entering, processing, or storing information in a computer or a computer system[24]. Computerization is about automation, mechanization, digitization, and conversion. Generally, it involves the digitization of entities or processes that are preconceived, predetermined, and well defined. In contrast, computation is about the exploration of indeterminate, vague, unclear, and often ill-defined processes; because of its exploratory nature, computation aims at emulating or extending the human intellect. It is about rationalization, reasoning, logic, algorithm, deduction, induction, extrapolation, exploration and estimation. In its manifold implications, it involves problem-solving, mental structures, cognition, simulation, and rule-based intelligence, to name a few.

The dominant mode of utilizing computers in architecture today is that of computerization; entities or processes that are already conceptualized in the designer's mind are entered, manipulated, or stored on a computer system. In contrast, computation or computing, as a computer-based design tool, is generally limited. The problem with this situation is that designers do not take advantage of the computational power of the computer. Instead some adventure into manipulations or criticisms of computer models as if they were products of computation. While research and development of software involves extensive computational techniques, mouse-based manipulations of 3D computer models are not necessarily acts of computation. For instance, it appears, from the current discourse that mouse-based manipulations of control points on NURBS-based surfaces are considered by some theorists to be acts of computing[25]. While the mathematical concept and software implementation of NURBS as surfaces is a product of applied numerical computation, the rearrangement of their control points through commercial software is simply an affine transformation, i.e. a translation.

When comparing contemporary practicing architects such as Thom Mayne, Frank Gehry, and Peter Eisenman it is necessary to overlook many significant and distinguishing differences in order to identify at least one common theme: the use of the computer as an exploratory formal tool and the increasing dependency of their work on computational methods. The most paradigmatic examples of the last ten years invest in computationally generated partis and diagrams. Through computation, architecture transcends itself beyond the common and predictable. In contrast, computerization provokes Whorfian effects: through the use of commercial applications and the dependency on their design possibilities, the designer's work is at risk of being dictated by the language-tools they use. By unknowingly converting to the constraints of a particular computer application's style, one runs the risk of being associated not with the cutting-edge research, but with a mannerism of "hi-tech" style.

A paradigm shift is defined as a gradual change in the collective way of thinking. It is the change of basic assumptions, values, goals, beliefs, expectations, theories, and knowledge. It is about transformation, transcendence, advancement, evolution, and transition. While paradigm shift is closely related to scientific advancements, its true effect is in the collective realization that a new theory or model requires understanding traditional concepts in new ways, rejecting old assumptions, and replacing them with new. For T.S. Kuhn[26], scientific revolutions occur during those periods where at least two paradigms coexist, one traditional and at least one new. The paradigms are incommensurable, as are the concepts used to understand and explain basic facts and beliefs. The two live in different worlds. The movement from the old to a new paradigm is called a *paradigm shift*.

Traditionally, the dominant paradigm for discussing and producing architecture has been that of human intuition and ingenuity. For the first time perhaps, a paradigm shift is being formulated that outweighs previous ones[27]. Algorithmic design employs methods and devices that have no precedent. If architecture is to embark into the alien world of algorithmic form, its design methods should also incorporate computational processes. If there is a form beyond comprehension it will lie within the algorithmic domain. While human intuition and ingenuity may be the starting point, the computational and combinatorial capabilities of computers must also be integrated.

In developing computer programs one is forced to question how people think and how designs evolve. In other words, computers must be acknowledged not only as machines for imitating what is understood, but also as vehicles for exploring what is not understood. The entire sequence of specifying computer operations is similar to that of human thinking. When designing software for natural language understanding, knowledge representation, inference, or learning, one is actually transferring to a machine processes of human thinking. The computer becomes a mirror of the human mind, and as such it reflects its thinking. Therefore, design can be explored as a mental process not only by observing human behavior, but also by observing the machine's behavior. To do this, it is necessary to perform individual operations with substantial independence; that is, the entire sequence of operations must be such that there is no human intervention from the time data is entered until the results are obtained and that design decision-making mechanisms be built into the machine itself. This does not mean that a "computer-designer" is to be created even though that may be desirable eventually. Rather, it suggests the attainment of independence in solving particular design problems. Thus, the designer can observe via the computer one's own decision-making process and compare it with that of others.

Originally the role of computers in architecture was to replicate human endeavors and to take the place of humans in the design process. Later the role shifted to create systems that would be intelligent assistants to designers, relieving them from the need to perform the more trivial tasks and augmenting their decision-making capabilities. Today, the roles of computers vary from drafting and modeling to form-based processing of architectural information. While the future of computers appears to include a variety of possible roles, it is worth exploring these roles in the context provided by the question: "Who designs?" If one takes the position that designing is not exclusively a human activity and that ideas exist independently of human beings, then it would be possible to design a computational mechanism which would associate those ideas.

Endnotes

[1]See Picon, A. and A. Ponte, *Architecture and the Sciences: Exchanging Metaphors*. Princeton NJ: Princeton Papers on Architecture, 2003, pp. 292–313.

[2]See Alexander, C., *Notes on the Synthesis of Form*. Cambridge: Harvard University Press, 1967.

[3]An extension of Boolean logic dealing with the concept of partial truth was introduced later as fuzzy logic.

4See Chomsky, N., *Syntactic Structures*. The Hague: Mouton and Company, 1957.

5See Yessios, C., "Formal languages for site planning," in C.M. Eastman (ed.), *Spatial Synthesis in Computer-Aided Building Design*. New York: Wiley, 1975.

6See Gill, A., *System Modeling and Control*. New York: John Wiley and Sons, 1978.

7As in Negroponte's "architecture machine" (1970), which could follow a procedure and, at the same time, could "discern and assimilate" conversational idiosyncrasies. This machine, after observing a user's behavior, could reinforce the dialogue by using a predictive model to respond in a manner consistent with personal behavior and idiosyncrasies. The dialogue would be so intimate, "that only mutual persuasion and compromise would bring about ideas" (Negroponte, 1970: 13). The role of the machine would be that of a close and wise friend assisting in the design process.

8See Eastman, C.M. and M. Henrion, *M. GLIDE: Language for a Design Information System*. Pittsburgh: Carnegie-Mellon University, Institute of Physical Planning, 1967.

9See Mitchell, W., "Vitruvius computatus," in W.F.E. Preiser (ed.), *Proceedings of EDRA 4 Conference*, Stroudsbourg: Dowden, Hutchinson and Ross, 1973.

10See Lafue, G.M.E., "Integrating language and database for CAD applications," *Computer Aided Design* 11(3), 1979 and Rasdorf, W.J. and A.R. Kutay, "Maintenance of integrity during concurrent access in a building design database," *Computer Aided Design* 16(4), 1982.

11See Leighton, N., *Computers in the Architectural Office*. New York: Van Nostrand Reinhold, 1984.

12See Ford, K., "In caesura," in *Eisenman Studios at GSD: 1983–85*. Cambridge: Harvard University Graduate School of Design, 1986, p. 35.

13See Stiny, G., "Computing with form and meaning in architecture," *Journal of Architectural Education* 39, 1985 and Flemming, U., "The role of shape grammars in the analysis and creation of design," *Proceedings of Symposium on Computability of Design at SUNY Buffalo*, December 1986.

14See Yessios, C., "A Fractal Studio," *ACADIA 87 Proceedings*. North Carolina State University, 1987, p. 7.

15Evans, R., "Not to be used for wrapping purposes," *AAFiles* 10, 1987, p. 70.

[16]See Terzidis, K., "Transformational design," Gainesville FL: ACADIA 1989 Proceedings, pp. 87–101.

[17]See Calinescu, M., *The Five Faces of Modernity*. Bloomington: Duke University Press, 1987.

[18]In Martin Heidegger's words: "Words and language are not just shells into which things are packed for spoken or written inter-course. In the word, in language, things first come to be and are. For this reason too, misuse of language in mere idle talk, in slogans and phrases, destroys our genuine relation to things." See Heigegger, M., *Introduction to Metaphysics*. New Haven: Yale University Press, 2000, p. 15.

[19]See Alexander, C., *Notes on the Synthesis of Form*. Cambridge: Harvard University Press, 1967 and Venturi, C., *Complexity and Contradiction in Architecture*, 2nd Edition. New York: Museum of Modern Art, 2002; also see Novak, M., "Computational composi-tions," ACADIA 88 Proceedings, pp. 5–30, Mitchell, W., *Logic of Architecture*. Cambridge: MIT Press, 1990 and Eisenmann P., "Visions unfolding: architecture in the age of electronic media," *Intelligente Ambiente, Ars Eletronica,* 1992; Frazer, J., *An Evolutionary Architecture*. London: Architectural Association, 1995 and Lynn, G., *Animate form*. New York: Princeton Architectural Press, 1999.

[20]Pierre Bézier (1910–1999), the French engineer and creator of the Bézier curves and surfaces that are now the basis of most computer-aided design systems, makes no reference to Gilles Deleuze (1925–1995) and vice versa, even though both lived in the same place (Paris) at the same time.

[21]See Lynn, G., *Animate Form*. New York: Princeton Architectural Press, 1999, pp. 20–21.

[22]Greg Lynn reveals that "because of the stigma and fear of releasing control of the design process to software, few architects have attempted to use the computer as a schematic, organizing and generative medium for design." See Lynn, G., *Animate Form*. New York: Princeton Architectural Press, 1999, p. 19.

[23]In response to this discrepancy, the ancient Greeks devised a "fair" method of acknowledgement of authorship. The Pythagorean theorem, the spiral of Archimedes, or the Euclidean geometry is an attempt to give proper credit to the authors regardless of the status of their subjects as either inventions or discoveries.

[24]In its colloquial sense, computerization refers to the process of furnishing with a computer or a computer system.

[25]See Cuff, D., "Digital pedagogy: an essay: one educator's thoughts on design software's profound effects on design thinking

and teaching," *Architectural Record*, September 2001. In this article, Cuff considers that computing is "one of the most important transformations of the contemporary profession" and that today "computing has become a populist skill."

[26]See Kuhn, T.S., "The structure of scientific revolutions," 3rd edition. University of Chicago, 1996.

[27]Peter Eisenman referred to the idea of an electronic paradigm shift in architecture in 1992. He wrote: "During the fifty years since the Second World War, a paradigm shift has taken place that should have profoundly affected architecture: this was the shift from the mechanical paradigm to the electronic one. This change can be simply understood by comparing the impact of the role of the human subject on such primary modes of reproduction as the photograph and the fax; the photograph within the mechanical paradigm, the fax within the electronic one." See Eisenman, P., "Visions unfolding: architecture in the age of electronic media," *Ars Eletronica,* 1992.

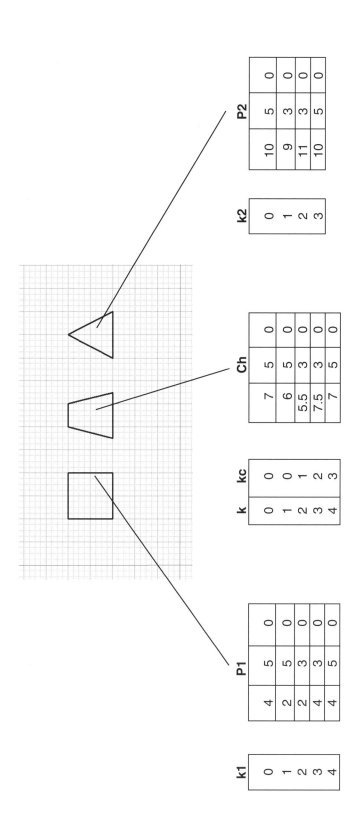

4 Scripts, algorithms, and other predicaments

An algorithm is a computational procedure for addressing a problem in a finite number of steps. It involves deduction, induction, abstraction, generalization, and structured logic. It is the systematic extraction of logical principles and the development of a generic solution plan. Algorithmic strategies utilize the search for repetitive patterns, universal principles, interchangeable modules, and inductive links. The intellectual power of an algorithm lies in its ability to infer new knowledge and to extend certain limits of the human intellect. An algorithm may be compared to the steps in a recipe; the steps of gathering the ingredients, preparing them, combining them, cooking, and serving are algorithmic steps in the preparation of food. Obviously, the number, size, and quality of ingredients, the sequence and timing of events, as well as the serving and presentation of the final product are key factors to a recipe. Theoretically, an algorithm is the abstraction of a process and serves as a sequential pattern that leads towards the accomplishment of a desired task. For instance, the algorithm for cooking potatoes may be composed of the following steps:

1. Peel
2. Boil
3. Cut
4. Serve

If the steps are reversed or one more step is added or deleted, alternative recipes may be created that produce different results. These results may be better, the same, or worse than the original intention. However, as in cooking, alterations, randomness, or accidents in the process may lead to new solutions, none of which was known in advance and whose newly emerged identity often differs significantly from the originally intended target. In these cases, the algorithm serves as a pattern of thought that helps in understanding the problem, addresses its possible solutions, and/or is a vehicle for defining new problems.

The common definition of the term algorithm involves the word *finite* as it relates to a number of distinguishable, countable, well-defined and therefore limited, bounded, or determinable series of steps. However, while such an assumption ensures that the description of a solution to the problem, i.e. an algorithm, is composed of finite steps this does not mean that the problem itself has to be finite, bounded, or deterministic. For instance, a common practice in the world of algorithms is something referred to as an "infinite loop" – such a situation is regarded as a misfortune and often results in a termination. While the steps that describe an infinite loop may be finite and specific, the resulting situation is indeterminate and infinite. For instance, the simple repetitive pattern defined through the following statements:

$$A = \text{false};$$

start:

$$\text{if A is false then A = true};$$

$$\text{if A is true then A = false};$$

go to start;

leads to an infinite cyclical argument where A changes between true and false with no end. Yet, the series of statements are indeed finite, well defined, and accurate. Consider now the following simple algorithm:

start:

$$A = \text{random number between 0 and 10};$$

$$\text{If A is greater than 5 then exit}$$

$$\text{Else go to start};$$

In this case, there is a temporary uncertainty about the generation and occurrence of a number greater than 5 to terminate the loop. While eventually such a possibility is almost certain, its time of occurrence is not necessarily so. The series of statements are finite yet lead to indeterminate, uncertain, and unpredictable behavior.

In the following sections of this chapter basic structures and processes of MEL scripting[1] will be introduced in order to understand, clarify, and illustrate some of the mechanisms, relationships, and connections behind the forms generated. This is not intended to be an exhaustive introduction to scripting but rather an indication of the potential and a point of reference for assessing the value of algorithms.

Variables

A variable is a symbolic representation of a changing data value. Variables can be created using letters preceded by a dollar sign. As long as there is no empty space a variable name should be valid. For example, $a, $sum, $value, $randomNumber are all valid names. Variables, once defined, are case sensitive, i.e. $temp is not the same as $Temp. Case sensitivity applies also to commands, i.e. move is not the same as Move, or polyCube is not the same as polycube.

To assign a value to a variable simply use the = sign and place the data value to the right side. For example, $a = 5 will assign 5 to variable $a, or $x = 3.5 will assign 3.5 to variable $x (until a new value is assigned). We distinguish two types of arithmetic data: integer numbers (whole) and float numbers (fractional).

A variable can also accept data from a command whose output may be unknown. For example, $r = rand(0,10) is a case where the output of a random process that creates random numbers between 0 and 10 will be assigned to $r. In this case, we will not know what the value of $r is until we print it out using the print command. For example,

$r = rand(0,10);

print $r;

These two sentences separated by a semi-colon (;) will assign a random number and print it on the screen.

Variable data types

We use variables to hold data. Variables can be of different types: if we hold whole numbers we called them integer variables and use the symbolic name **int**, if hold characters we call them strings and use the name **string**. There are four variable data types

Table 4.1 Variable data types

Type	Description	Example
int	Integer numbers	−1, 0, 4, 100
float	Fractional numbers	2.3, −0.1, 23.45
string	Characters and words	"a," "apple," "12"
vector	3D coordinates	<<1.1,2.2,4.1>>, <<0,0,0>>

Operations

We have two types of operation: arithmetic and logical. Arithmetic operations are addition (+), subtraction (−), multiplication (*), and division (/). There is also an operation called remainder (%) and returns the remainder of the division between two numbers. For example,

$a = 5;

$b = 2;

$c = $a + $b;

In this case $c will become 7. In the following example:

$c = $a % $b;

$c will become be 1, because 5 divided by 2 is 2 and the remainder is 1. In brief:

Table 4.2 Arithmetic operations

Operator	Use	Description
+	op1 + op2	Adds op1 and op2
−	op1 − op2	Subtracts op2 from op1
*	op1 * op2	Multiplies op1 by op2
/	op1 / op2	Divides op1 by op2
%	op1 % op2	Computes the remainder of dividing op1 by op2

Logical operations are those that involve the truth or falsity of the comparison between two variables. Those operations are greater (>), greater or equal (>=), equal (==), not equal (!=), less (<), and less or equal (<=). The logical operation is performed using the command **if** followed by parentheses containing the logical operation. As an alternative condition we use the **else** command. For example, the statement:

```
$a=3;

$b=4;

if($a > $b) {

    print $a;

}

else {

    print $b;

}
```

The "if" statement tests the truthfulness of the operation and if it is true executes the following commands enclosed between the curly brackets { and }. In general, curly brackets group statements that need to be executed sequentially as a group. In the following example we will determine the truthfulness of a logical statement whose operand data is unknown.

```
$r1 = rand(0,10);

$r2 = rand(0,10);

if($r1 == $r2){

    print $r1;

}
```

The "if" statement here is used to determine whether the random number $r1 is equal to the random number $r2. Notice that the equality test uses the symbol == instead of the data assignment symbol =.

Table 4.3 Logical operations

Operator	Use	Returns true if
>	op1 > op2	op1 is greater than op2
>=	op1 >= op2	op1 is greater than or equal to op2
<	op1 < op2	op1 is less than op2
<=	op1 <= op2	op1 is less than or equal to op2
==	op1 == op2	op1 and op2 are equal
!=	op1 != op2	op1 and op2 are not equal

Repetition

A repetition statement is referred to as a loop. It consists of the command **for** followed by parentheses containing three parts: an initial condition; a termination condition; and a pace of repetition. For example,

```
for($i=0; $i<10; $i=$i+1){

    print $i;

}
```

is a loop that will initiate a variable $i to 0, terminate when the variable is 10, and increment in steps of 1. At each loop, it will print out the value of $i. The result would be

```
0123456789
```

Notice that the loop starts at 0 and exits at 10, so 9 is the last printed element. However, as a total, the printed elements are 10.

The statement $i = $i + 1 can be also expressed as $i++. The ++ symbol means "add 1 to ...." In contrast the symbol −− means "subtract 1 from ...." So, below are various loops:

```
for($i=0; $i<20; $++)

for($i=10; $i>0; $i−−)

for($x=−10; $x<10; $x=$x+2)
```

The first loop will start at 0, stop at 20 and increment by 1. The second loop will start at 10, stop at 0, and decrement by 1. The third loop will start at −10, stop at 10, and increment by 2.

There are two commands associated with loops: **continue** and **break**. "Continue" will skip one loop and "break" will exit the whole loop. For example, the following loop:

```
for($i=0; $i<20; $i++){
    if($i==4)continue;
    if($i>7) break;
    print $i;
}
```

will produce the following printout: 0123567. 4 is skipped and after 7 the loop is abandoned.

By using simple arithmetic operations one can produce various number patterns. For instance,

```
for($i=0; $i<20; $i++){
    $x = $i/2;
    print $x;
};
```

will produce the following number pattern (notice that $i is integer so fractional values will be omitted)

00112233445566778899...

Similarly, the following formulas will result in the following number patterns:

Table 4.4 Repetition patterns

Formula	Result
$x = $i/3;	00011122233344455566
$x = $i/4;	00001111222233334444
$x = ($i+1)/2;	01122334455667788 9910
$x = ($i+2)/2;	11223344556677889910 10
$x = $i%2;	01010101010101010101
$x = $i%3;	01201201201201201201
$x = $i%4;	01230123012301230123
$x = ($i+1)%4;	12301230123012301230
$x = ($i+2)%4;	23012301230123012301
$x = ($i/2)%2;	00110011001100110011
$x = ($i/3)%2;	00011100011100011100
$x = ($i/4)%2;	00112233001122330011

Arrays

An array is an ordered set of data. We can have arrays of integers, floats, strings etc. We define an array by using the [] symbol. For example:

```
int $evenNumbers[];

string $listOfNames[5];
```

The above arrays define 0 and 5 elements respectively. An array can be initialized with data values using the {} operation. For example:

```
int $numbers[4] = {3, 5, 2, 1};

float $temperatures[6] = {103.4, 101.0, 99.3, 98.2,
                           97.3, 98.1};

string $colors[3] = {"brown", "red", "green"};
```

To extract the value of an array member we use an index starting from 0. So, in the following example:

```
int $numbers[4] = {3, 5, 2, 1};

print($numbers[0]);          //should be 3

print($numbers[3]);          //should be 1
```

Once we create an array we can fill it with data and then access them. For example:

```
int $evenNumbers[];

for($i=0; $i<50; $i++){

          $evenNumbers[$i] = $i * 2;

}

print($evenNumbers[31]);    //should be 62
```

The command size() returns the size of an array as an integer number. The commands clear() and sort() will clear and sort arrays respectively. For example:

```
int $x[30];

print(size($x));          //will be 30

clear($x);

print(size($x));          //will be 0
```

Geometrical objects and transformations

Maya has geometrical objects such as curves, surfaces or solids that have names in MEL. For example, a curve is called "curve," a NURBS surface is called "nurbsPlane," a sphere is called "sphere," or a polygonal cube is called "polyCube." For example, to create a sphere, the command "sphere," typed in the editor, will generate a default sphere. These geometrical commands are listed in the **Help->MEL Command Reference**. To modify the parameters of any geometrical object we use modifiers called flags that are also listed in the MEL command reference. For example, the command:

sphere –r 5;

or

polyCube –w 1 –d 0.5 –h 3;

will create a sphere of radius 5 and a polygonal cube of width 1, depth 0.5, and height 3. Each flag is defined by a minus sign, a name (or initial) and a data value, i.e. "–w 1" means width of 1 unit.

By default all objects are situated at the 0,0,0 origin at the object's center. To change the location, orientation, or size we use the **move**, **rotate** and **scale** commands. Each command takes three numbers that represent the x, y, and z value of the transformation. For example,

sphere –r 1

move 10 3 5.5

rotate 30 0 45

scale 1 2 1

will create a sphere of radius 1 and then move it at location 10, 3, 5.5, then rotate it by 30 degrees in the x direction, 0 degrees in the y direction and 45 degrees in the z direction and finally scale the object twice in the y direction but leave it intact in the other directions (1 is the identity operator for scaling). Each transformation also has modifier flags associated with the transformation. The most important flag is –r (–relative) which moves, rotates, or translates an object relative to its previous location. So, for example, in the previous example:

move –r 10 3 5.5

will move the sphere 10, 3, 5.5 units away from its previous position to location 20 6 11 (as opposed to the absolute location of 10,3,5.5 which is the default state when no flag is used).

Attributes

A geometrical object may be composed of subelements, i.e. a polygon-based (polyCube) is composed of faces, edges, and vertices and a NURBS-based (cube) surface composed of isoparms and control points. The location of these elements can be addressed using the . (=dot) separator in the form

Object.element

For example, for a polyCube named MyCube, we can extract its first vertex in the following manner:

$p = pointPosition MyCube.vtx[0];

The pointPosition command returns the actual coordinates of the point in Cartesian space.

To get the attributes associated with an object we use the getAttr command. So

$r = getAttr MyCube.rotate

will return the xyz rotational angles of MyCube in the variable $r. These values, in turn, can be extracted as

float $rx = $r[0];

float $ry = $r[1];

float $rz = $r[2];

In this case $r is an array with three elements that correspond to the values of xyz in the order 012.

Similarly, the xyz translational coordinates of MyCube can be obtained using the command

$t = getAttr MyCube.translate

This array $t holds the xyz coordinates of the center of the object. To get the actual location of each vertex we use the pointPosition command (above).

Sometimes the name of an object may be a variable, i.e. $object_name. If we use the getAttr command the system will return an error because the following

```
$t = getAttr $object_name.translate
```

is confusing. So, instead we create the actual command as a string and then execute it using the eval command:

```
$t = eval("getAttr" + $object_name + ".translate");
```

Sequential transformation

Using loops, geometrical objects, and transformations we can place objects sequentially creating rhythm, repetition, or progression. For example, the following code will generate 12 cubes of half-unit and place them in equal distance of 2 units in the x direction:

```
for($x=0; $x<12; $x++){
    polyCube –w 0.5 –d 0.5 –h 0.5;
    move ($x*2) 0 0;
}
```

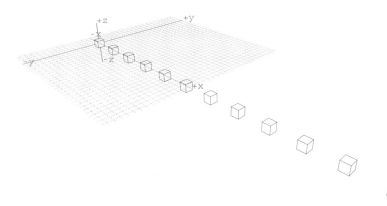

4.1
Linear repetition

Similarly, the following code will generate a series of 15 cubes, scale them along the z axis, move them 1 unit apart, and progressively rotate them by 10 degrees in the x direction:

```
for($x=0; $x<15; $x++){
        polyCube –w 1 –d 1 –h 1;
        move ($x) 0 0;
        scale 0.5 0.5 5;
        rotate ($x*10) 0 0;
}
```

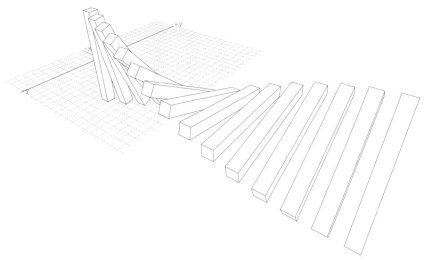

4.2
Rotational progression

We can also introduce randomness in the process by adding (or subtracting) a randomly generated value. For example, the following code will create 20 sequential cubes whose height will be random:

```
for($x=0; $x<20; $x++){
$r = rand(-3, 3);
        polyCube –w 1 –d 1 –h (5+$r);
        move ($x*2) 0 0;
}
```

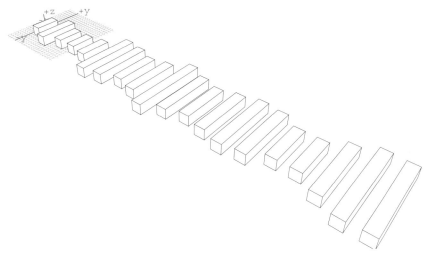

4.3
Scaling variations

The remainder operation(%) can also be used to create repetition at variable distances. Because the remainder of the division of any number by a divisor will always be 0 if the divisor is divided exactly we can use this property to create rhythm. For example:

```
for($x=0; $x<40; $x++){

        if($x%5==0) continue;

        polyCube –w 1 –d 1 –h 1;

        move ($x*2) 0 0;

    }
```

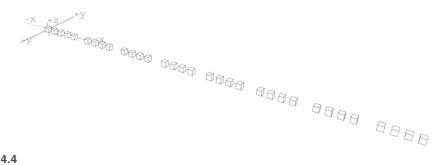

4.4
Interrupted progression

will skip one every five cubes because the remainder of the division of $x with 5 is 0 every time $x is a multiple of 5.

Loops can occur in one direction, but also in two or three directions. For example, the following code:

```
for($y=0; $y<10; $y++){
    for($x=0; $x<10; $x++){
        polyCube –w 1 –d 1 –h 1;
        move ($x*2) ($y*2) 0;
    }
}
```

will produce a series of rows of cubes in the x direction (as seen in the inner x loop) but then will produce sequences of rows in the y direction (as seen in the outer y loop).

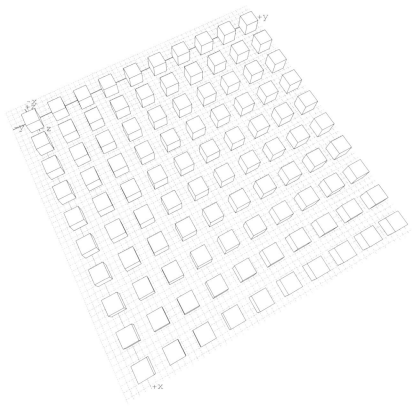

4.5
A two-dimensional grid

The command **rand**($min, $max) will create a random number between $min and $max. For example:

$r = rand(–5, 5)

will create a random fractional number (i.e. 2.1 or –4.1) between –5 and 5.

Randomness can always be introduced as a deviation from an orderly placement. For example, adding a random number to an existing location will produce the following code and effect:

```
for($y=0; $y<10; $y++){

    for($x=0; $x<10; $x++){

        polyCube –w 1 –d 1 –h 1;

        $r = rand(–0.2, 0.2);

        move (($x+$r)*2) (($y+$r)*2) 0;

    }

}
```

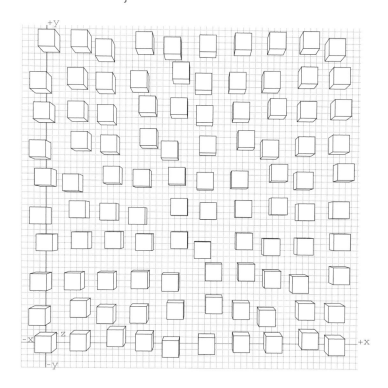

4.6
A random disturbance of a two-dimensional grid

The amount of randomness added to an orderly pattern can be subtle enough to create a balanced composition of order and disorder.

Multi-Booleans

Geometric Boolean operations are used to articulate the presence or absence of material substances. Theoretically, there are three boolean operations, OR, AND, and NOT, that correspond to logical operations. However, in the context of solid objects, these operations correspond to union, intersection, and difference. While the minimum operands

4.7
Order and randomness (class project by M. Snyder for course GSD2311 taught by Kostas Terzidis in Fall 2005 at Harvard University)

4.8
Disturbed landscape (class project by C. Shusta for course GSD2311 taught by Kostas Terzidis in Fall 2005 at Harvard University)

for these operations are always two, combination or repetitive application of the operations can result in complicated forms.

A union B   A intersection B   A difference B   B difference A

4.9
Boolean operations

Traditionally, architects have maintained a logic of accumulative progression during the design process. Because of the artificial nature of design, architects traditionally follow a bottom-up approach where elements are composed into objects, and objects into groups to form structures, systems, and buildings. Iakov Chernikov and other constructivists, for example, elaborated on the combination of forms, using the basic concepts of "constructive combinations," such as combination, assemblage, penetration, mounting, integrating, coupling, interlacing, and so on, both statically and dynamically, using hard or soft materials. These concepts constitute a Boolean design language, one having the advantage of combining forms in a manner familiar to architects.

The following code shows a simple method to union multiple objects and to difference one object from multiple objects creating holes or niches:

```
1   seed(5.); //optional, in order to repeat randomness
2
3   for($i=0; $i<20; $i++){
4           $name = "MyObject" + $i;
5           polyCube -name $name;
6           move (rand(-.5,.5)) (rand(-.5,.5)) (rand(-.5,.5));
7           scale (rand(2.5,3.5)) (rand(2.5,3.5)) (rand(2.5,3.5));
```

```
8    } //for i

9

10

11   polyBoolOp -op 1 -name MyResult1 MyObject0 MyObject1; //union the first
     two objects

12

13   for($next=2; $next <20; $next++){ // go for the rest

14         $obj_next = "MyObject" + $next; //define the next object

15         $previous = $next - 1;

16         $obj_previous = "MyResult" + $previous;

17         $result = "MyResult" + $next; //define the previous object

18         polyBoolOp -op 1 -name $result $obj_previous $obj_next; //union
           the previous with the next

19   }// for next

20

21         rename MyResult19 MyResult0; //rename the object to start the difference
           process

22

23   for ($i=0; $i<20; $i++) { //for 30 objects to be differences (i.e. holes)

24               //create a cylinder to be used for subtraction (difference)

25               polyCylinder -n ("MyCylinder" + $i) -h (rand(8,9)) -r (rand (.05,.1));

26               move (rand(-1,1)) (rand(-1,1)) (rand(-1,1)); //move anywhere within
                 the target body

27               //subtract (difference) the previous with the next

28               eval ("polyBoolOp -op 2 -n MyResult" + ($i +1) + "MyResult" +
                 $i + "MyCylinder" + $i);

29         }; //for i
```

The first line of the code uses the command seed that initializes a sequence of random numbers. The statement is optional and should be used to produce the exact same effect of random sequences. Lines 3 to 8 are a description of creating 20 cubes of various shapes that overlap one another. At line 11 we union the first two objects (i.e. MyObject0 and MyObject1) and create a combined object called MyResult1. We then loop through the rest of the objects (i.e. 2 to 20) to union every object with the next one. At each step we create a resulting object called MyResult which is used as the previous object.

At line 21 we are renaming the last and only object in the scene which is the result of the combined union. We call it MyResult0. This object will be used as a target for difference operations to follow.

We loop through 20 times and create long cylinders that are dispersed so that they can penetrate throughout the target object MyResult0. We then subtract each cylinder from the target object and then use the new object created to subtract from it again.

The results of these operations are shown in Figures 4.10 and 4.11.

Similarly, a series of spheres can be subtracted from the cube or a series of cubes can be subtracted from a cylinder. While the original objects are subtracted and therefore deleted, their presence is still visible through the mold that reflects their absence. Absence becomes the state of not being present.

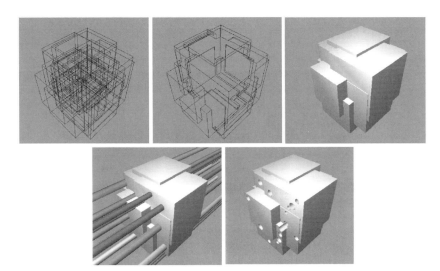

4.10
Union of multiple cubes (top) and subtraction of multiple cylinders (bottom)

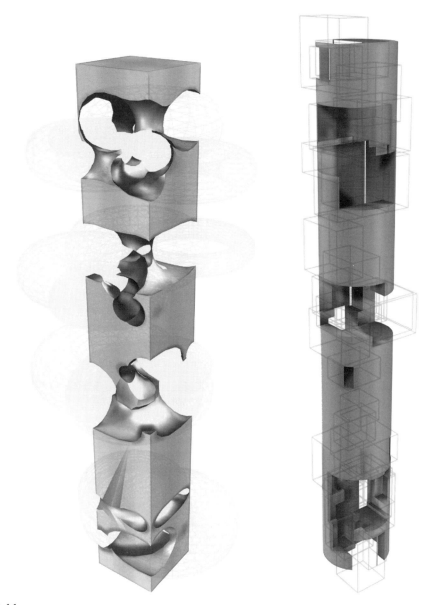

4.11
Subtracted objects are still present through their absence (class project by C. Shusta for course GSD2311 taught by Kostas Terzidis in Fall 2005 at Harvard University)

Stochastic search

A stochastic search is defined here as a random search in space until a given condition is met. For instance, the placement of toys in a playpen so that each toy does not overlap another and they all fit within the limits of the playpen can be addressed with a stochastic search. The algorithm will work as follows:

```
while(no more toys left to place){

        choose randomly a position (rx, ry) within the playpen

        compare it with all previous toy locations

        is there an overlap? (if no then place the
        toy at (rx, ry))

}
```

This algorithm can use used to place objects within a site so that there is no overlap (or some other criterion is satisfied). In the following code, a series of 100 cubes is placed within an area of 10×10.

1	**for($i=0; $i<100; $i++){** //for all objects
2	
3	**$name = "MyCube" + $i;** //create a series name
4	**polyCube -w 1 -d 1 -h 1 -name $name;** //make a cube
5	
6	**$range = 10;** //define a range
7	**$sv=0;** //set a safety valve to avoid infinite loops
8	**while(true){** //search forever
9	**$rx = rand(-$range,$range);** //get a random x position (dart)
10	**$ry = rand(-$range,$range);** //get a random x position
11	**$overlap = false;** //set a flag a false (until proof of the opposite)
12	**for($j=0; $j<$i; $j++){** //loop through all the previous elements
13	**$name = "MyCube" + $j;** //get a previous name
14	**$px = eval("getAttr "+ $name + ".translateX");** //get the x location of the previous
15	**$py = eval("getAttr "+ $name + ".translateY");** //get the y location of the previous

fi   w   fj

16   **$diffx = abs((float)($rx-$px));** *//get the x distance between previous and candidate*

17   **$diffy = abs((float)($ry-$py));** *//get the y distance between previous and candidate*

18   **if($diffx < 1. && $diffy < 1.)** *// if x and y distance is less than tolerance (i.e. 1)*

19   **$overlap = true;** *//set the flag*

20   – **}** *//for j again*

21   **if($overlap==false){** *//if there is no overlap*

22   **move $rx $ry 0;** *// move the cube in the location (the position satisfies the criterion)*

23   **textCurves -f "Courier" -t $i;** *// make a label with its serial number to identify it*

24   **move $rx $ry 0;** *// move the label to the middle of the new cube*

25   **scale -r 0.1 0.1 0.1;** *// scale the label*

26   **break;** *//exit the while loop*

27   **}**

28   **$sv++;if($sv >1000){ print ("not found\n");break;}** *//if 1000 unsuccessful attempts are made exit*

29   – **}**//while (again)

30

31 **};** //for $i

The algorithm starts with an outer loop where a hundred cubes are to be placed. First, each cube is named sequentially as MyCube0, MyCube1, MyCube2, etc. and then created (lines 3 and 4). A range is defined as 10 and a counter $sv is initialized to be used later in order to avoid infinite loops (to be called here a safety valve). Then, in lines 9 and 10 we create random locations and x and y between negative and positive ranges. If flag is being set to false that will be used later to determine whether there's an overlap or not. Now, we need to loop back through all the objects that have been created already (line 12). So, we get the name of each previous cube and use it to extract the translational value in both x and y, which we use to determine the distance between the previous and the candidate. In other words, given a random location we need to determine whether positioning a cube will overlap any of the previous cubes. In line 18 we test to see whether the difference is enough to allow a cube to be placed in between. If the distance is not enough then set the flag to be true. Else we set the flag to false. We continue looping for all the objects and if the flag continues to be false (i.e. there is no overlap) we move the cube at the candidate random location (line 22). The next three lines of code create 3D text with the number of the cube (for identification purposes) and then break out of the while loop. Line 28 is referred to as a "safety valve" and its purpose is to force an exit to the loop if an infinite loop situation occurs. The counter $sv increases by one at each attempt, so if the number of unsuccessful attempts exceeds 1000 (or any sufficiently large number) then the system is forced to exit the loop.

Figure 4.12 shows the placement of a hundred troops in an area of 10 × 10 without overlaps.

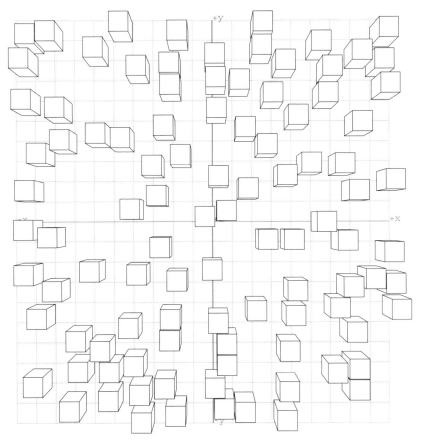

4.12
Distribution of 100 cubes within a 10 × 10 site with no overlap

Of course, this algorithm can be modified to allow only overlaps by reversing the logic, or the conditions for placement can be so complex that they can satisfy various architectural conditions (i.e. public space, sun exposure, zoning envelope, etc.).

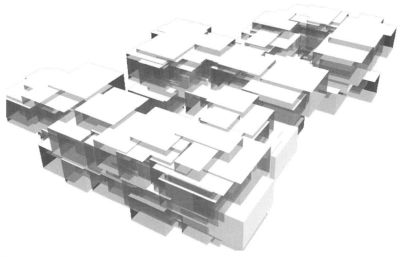

4.13
A housing development that uses stochastic search to determine the location of its units

Fractals

A fractal is a geometric object generated by a repeating pattern, in a typically recursive or iterative process. Usually, the outcome shape can be divided into parts, each of which is similar to the original shape. Fractals are said to possess infinite detail, and some of them have a self-similar structure that occurs at different levels of magnification. The term fractal was coined in 1975 by Benoît Mandelbrot, from the Latin word *fractus* or *broken*.

In a fractal process, there are at least two shapes: a base and a generator. In each iteration, the generator replaces each segment of the base shape. Theoretically this process continues infinitely. The algorithm to create fractals consists of a basic procedure that fits a shape between two points. The process of fitting involves scaling, rotation, and translation of the generator to fit between two points of a segment of the base. The following code shows the procedure:

```
1  proc fit (vector $start, vector $end, vector $shape[]){
2
3      // make a curve out of the array points in shape[]
4      string $points = ""; //create an empty string
5      $point = $shape[0]; //get the first point
6
7      for($i=0; $i< size($shape); $i++){      //for all points of the shape
8          $point = $shape[($i)];      //extract a point
9          $points += " -p " + $point; //add it to the string
10     }
11     eval("curve -d 1 " + $points); //create a curve out of the input points
       in $shape[]
12
13     //scale to fit
14     $temp_end = $end - $start;   // move the points to the origin
15     float $mag = mag($temp_end); // get the magnitude of their length
16     float $amag = mag($point);   // get the magnitude of the length of the
       base segment
17     float $scale_factor = $mag/$amag; //get the scaling factor
18     scale $scale_factor $scale_factor $scale_factor;// scale
19
20     //rotate to fit
21     float $anglex = atan2d($temp_end.y,$temp_end.x); //atan2d gives the
       angle
22     rotate 0 0 $anglex;// rotate      //from the origin to a point
23
24     //move to fit
25     move ($start.x) ($start.y) ($start.z); // move back to the original location
26
27     refresh; //refresh the screen to see the replacement as it happens
28 } //procedure end
```

The procedure called fit takes as input a point called $start, a point called $end, and an array of points that define the shape to be fitted. Each point is defined here as a vector. A vector is a data type that contains three float numbers for x, y, and z, which can be extracted using the dot operator, i.e. for a vector called $start we have $x = $start.x; $y = $start.y; and $z = $start.z.

First, we create an empty string to be filled with points that will later on define a curve. In line 5 we extract the first point of the input shape (to be used later in line 16). Then we loop through all the points of the input shape, extract each point and put them into the variable $point, and concatenate each point to the string $points (lines 8 and 9). The command size() is used here to extract the size of the array $shape. After the loop is done, we create a curve of dimension one (a polyline). This is the generator shape that will be fitted between points $start and $end.

Next we scale the curve to fit between the two points. In line 14 we subtract start from end thus bringing the gap to be fitted to the origin (0,0,0). We then get the magnitude of the gap as well as the magnitude of the length of the curve to be fitted. We divide the two magnitudes attending a factor for scale. We use that factor to scale the curve.

Then we rotate the curve by an angle. This angle points at the direction of the end point. The command atan2d returns the angle from the origin to a point. In this case, the point is the offset end point $temp_end. Finally, we move the point back to its original location. (The refresh command is used here as an effect so that we can see the replacement as it happens.)

The next procedure is the main one where the fractal operation is called (the identifier **global** allows it to be called from everywhere and at anytime):

```
1   global proc fractal(){
2
3       vector $generator[]; //make an array for the generator
4       $generator = getPoints("curve1"); //populate the array with the curve1
        (generator) points
5       vector $base[]; //make an array for the base
```

```
6
7       string $list[];
8       $list = eval("ls -transforms \"curve*\""); //returns an array with the names of
9                                    //all objects in the scene that match the
                                     word "curve"
10
11      for($j = 1; $j<size($list); $j++){ //we start at 1 because 0 is the generator
12              $base_name = $list[($j)];
13
14              $base = getPoints($base_name); //get the points
15              //once we have the points we erase the shape since we will replace it
16              eval("delete " + $base_name);
17
18              for($i=0; $i<(size($base)-1); $i++)
19                      //replace the current (i) and next (i+1) points with the
                        generator's array
20                      fit($base[$i], $base[($i+1)], $generator);
21      } //for j
22  } // procedure end
```

The fractal procedure starts by defining two main arrays: generator and base where the points of the generator and base shape will be stored respectively. In line 4 a procedure called getPoints is called that will extract the points from a shape and put them in an array (this procedure will be defined later). At this point we assume

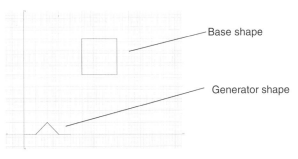

4.14
A base and a generator shape

that we have created two curves (of dimension 1) that are called by default names curve1 (generator) and curve2 (base). It is important that the generator starts at the origin and that the y-axis is upwards.

In line 8 we use this command to extract all the objects in the scene that match the word *curve*. These curves will be replaced by the generator. So, in line 11 we loop through all the curves except the first one because that is the generator. We extract their name and then extract their points and put them in an array called $base. Once we are done we delete the base shape because it is not needed anymore. We then loop through all the points of each segment of the base shape and replace it with the generator (line 20).

The next procedure extracts the points of a given curve and puts them (populates) into an array which it then returns as an array of vectors:

```
1    proc vector[] getPoints(string $curve_name){

2

3        //get the number of spans

4        $numSpans = eval("getAttr " + $curve_name + ".spans");

5        vector $points[]; //make a vector array to collect the points

6

7        for($i=0; $i<($numSpans+1); $i++){

8            $point = eval("pointPosition " + $curve_name + ".cv[" +
             $i   + "]");
             //get the cvs

9            float $x = $point[0];

10           float $y = $point[1];

11           float $z = $point[2];

12           vector $v = <<$x, $y, $z>>;

13           $points[$i] = $v; //store the values in points[]

14       } //for i

15       return $points; //return the array

16   } //procedure end
```

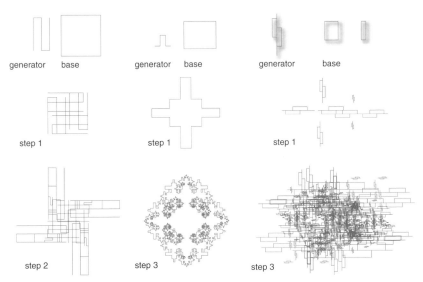

4.15
Various fractals (class project by K. Hopkins for course GSD2311 taught by Kostas Terzidis in Fall 2005 at Harvard University)

First, the number of points (i.e. spans) need to be extracted. We use the geAttr command to extract the number of spans (line 4), then we loop through all the spans to extract the position of each control point. We put these coordinates into a vector array and return it.

Below are some examples using fractals:

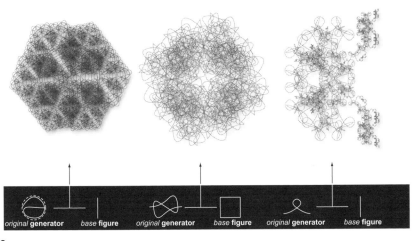

4.16
Fractals with curves (class project by K. Takeuchi for course GSD2311 taught by Kostas Terzidis in Fall 2005 at Harvard University)

Cellular automata

A cellular automaton (plural: cellular automata) is a discrete model that consists of a finite, regular grid of cells, each in one of a finite number of states. Time is also discrete, and the state of a cell at a time slice is a function of the state of a finite number of cells called the neighborhood at the previous time slice. Every cell exhibits a local behavior based on a rule(s) applied which in turn is based on values in its neighborhood. Each time the rules are applied to the whole grid a new generation is produced.

4.17
An 8-neighborhood

While cellular automata (CA) were developed originally to describe organic self-replicating systems, their structure and behavior were also useful in addressing architectural, land-scape, and urban design problems. From vernacular settle-ments and social interaction to material behavior and air circulation, CA may provide interesting interpretations of urban and architectural phenomena. The basic idea behind CA is not to describe a complex system with complex equa-tions, but to let the complexity emerge by interaction of simple individuals following simple rules. Typical features of CA include: absence of external control (autonomy), sym-metry breaking (loss of freedom/heterogeneity), global order (emergence from local interactions), self-maintenance (repair/reproduction metabolisms), adaptation (functional-ity/tracking of external variations), complexity (multiple con-current values or objectives), and hierarchy (multiple nested self-organized levels).

The following algorithm was developed as a kernel to implement cellular automata for architectural purposes:

```
1      int $xmax = 40;

2      int $ymax = 40;

3

4  //create the lattice of cells
```

```
5   for($x=0; $x<$xmax; $x++) // loop in x-direction

6           for($y=0; $y<$ymax; $y++){ // loop in y-direction

7                polyPlane -ax 0 0 1 -w 1 -h 1 -sx 1 -sy 1 -name ("MyPlane" +
                 $x + "x" + $y);

8                move $x $y 0;

9                }

10  //disurb it

11  for($x=0; $x<$xmax; $x++) // loop in x-direction

12          for($y=0; $y<$ymax; $y++){ // loop in y-direction

13               $name = ("MyPlane" + $x + "x" + $y);

14               if(rand(2.) >1.) eval("setAttr "+$name+".visibility 0");
                 //show or hide

15               }

16

17  int $status[]; //keep a memory of the current state of each cell

18

19  for($gen=0; $gen<10; $gen++) { //the number of trials (generations)

20

21              //first pass: collect information from the neighbors

22              int $idx = 0; //initialize a counter

23              for($x=1; $x<$xmax-1; $x++) // loop in x-direction

24                   for($y=1; $y<$ymax-1; $y++){ // loop in y-direction

25                        $name = ("MyPlane" + $x + "x" + $y);

26                        $visible = 0.;

27                        for($i=-1; $i<=1; $i++) // loop by three positions

28                             for($j=-1; $j<=1; $j++){ // loop by
                              three positions

29                                  if($i==0 && $j==0)continue;
                                    // exclude the cell itself

30                                  $nameNeighbor = ("MyPlane"
                                    + ($x+$i) + "x" + ($y+$j));

31                                  $v = eval("getAttr
                                    "+$nameNeighbor+" .visibility");
                                    //get value
```

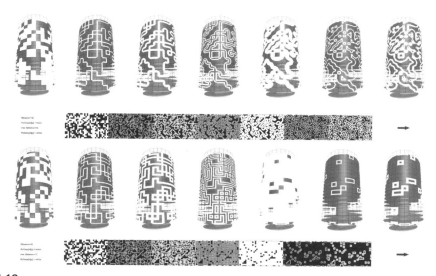

4.18
Cellular automata as an LCD display wrapped around a building (class project by N. Anderson for course GSD2311 taught by Kostas Terzidis in Fall 2005 at Harvard University)

Architectural morphing preserves the structural integrity of the objects involved, that is, an object changes into another object as a single entity. A cube, for instance, may be gradually transformed into a pyramid. From the viewer's point of view, there are always two objects: *the original (or source),* to which transformation is applied, and the *destination object (or target),* which is the object one will get at the final step of the transformation. However, theoretically, there is only one object, which is transformed from one state (original) into another (destination). This object combines characteristics of both

4.19
Cellular automata maze (class project by M. Snyder for course GSD2311 taught by Kostas Terzidis in Fall 2005 at Harvard University)

MORPHING 2
ENTITIES TOGETHER
TO CREATE SOMETHING
UNEXPECTED

parent objects, which are involved in the transformation and is called a *hybrid object*. This object is actually composed of the topology of one object and the geometry of the other. It is an object in disguise. Although it is topologically identical to the one parent it resembles the geometry of the other parent.

TAKING THE
IDENTITITY OF
BOTH OBJECTS

↓

BECOME A NEW
TYPOLOGY.

Interpolation is a method for estimating values that lie between two known values[2]. The hybrid object derives its structure from its parents through formal interpolations. While it is easy to derive hybrid children from isomorphic parents, a challenge arises for heteromorphic parents. In an isomorphic transformation, a one-to-one correspondence applies between the elements of the two parent sets, such that the result of an operation on elements of one set corresponds to the result of the analogous operation on their images in the other set. In the case of heteromorphism, the lack of homogeneity among the parents leads necessarily to a selective process of omissions and inclusion of elements between the two sets. The guiding principle in this mapping process is the preservation of the topological and geometrical properties of the hybrid object. For instance, in the case of a square mapped to a triangle, the addition of a fourth point to the triangle preserves the topology of the square and yet its disguised location preserves the geometrical appearance of the triangle.

In the example in Figure 4.20, a square is mapped to a triangle: the hybrid child is a four-sided polygon in which two

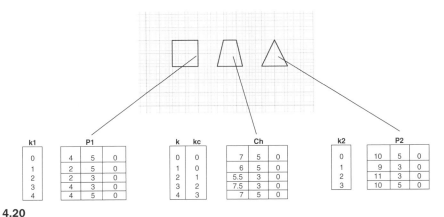

k1	P1		
0	4	5	0
1	2	5	0
2	2	3	0
3	4	3	0
4	4	5	0

k	kc	Ch		
0	0	7	5	0
1	0	6	5	0
2	1	5.5	3	0
3	2	7.5	3	0
4	3	7	5	0

k2	P2		
0	10	5	0
1	9	3	0
2	11	3	0
3	10	5	0

4.20
The coordinates of the parents and the hybrid child

of the vertices overlap and are ordered to form a triangle. The problem here is to map two counters so that when the one is counting points from one object to another the counter kc should skip points from the other object. For example, if the one counter k increments as 01234 the counter kc should increment as 00123 (or 01123 or 01223 or 01233). To obtain such behavior, we use the function kc = k/(p1/p2) or kc = k/(p2/p1).

```
1  global proc hybrid(string $parent1, string $parent2, float $ratio){

2

3      int $p1pnts = eval("getAttr "+ $parent1 +".spans"); //number of
       points of parent 1

4      int $p2pnts = eval("getAttr "+ $parent2 +".spans"); //number of points of
       parent 2

5      int $degree = eval("getAttr "+ $parent2 +".degree");

6      int $numpoints = max($p1pnts, $p2pnts);   //child has the number of
       points of the biggest parent

7      int $k1 = 0; // counter 1

8      int $k2 = 0; // counter 2

9

10     string $spoints = "";   //string to hold curve values

11     float $point[];

12

13     for($k=0; $k<($numpoints+1); $k++){

14             if($p1pnts>=$p2pnts){   //if p1 is greater than p2

15                     $k1 = $k;                          //counter 1 remains
                       as is

16                     $k2 = $k/(($p1pnts*1.)/($p2pnts*1.)); }   //counter 2
                       must be adjusted

17             else {    //if p2 is greater than p1

18                     $k1 = $k/(($p2pnts*1.)/($p1pnts*1.));      //counter 1
                       must be adjusted

19                     $k2 = $k; }   //counter 2 remains as is
```

```
20          // interpolate the values of the child relative to the parents
21          $p1 = eval("pointPosition "+ $parent1 +" .cv["+$k1+"] "); //get
            parent 1's points
22          $p2 = eval("pointPosition "+ $parent2 +" .cv["+$k2+"] "); //get
            parent 2's points
23          for($j=0; $j<3; $j++)
24                  $point[$j] = $p1[$j] + $ratio * ($p2[$j] - $p1[$j]);
25                  $spoints += " -p " + $point[0] + " " + $point[1] + "
                    " + $point[2]; //assign child pnts
26  }
27
28  eval("curve -d " + $degree + " " + $spoints ); //the child
    curve
29
30  }
```

The procedure hybrid takes as input the two parents' names and the ratio of interpolated steps. First, we extract the number of points of the two parents and their degree (and this case we're looking at curves). The number of points of the child object will be equal to the number of points of the largest parent. We then initialized two counters $k1 and $k2, a string $spoints to hold the curve values, and an array of floats called $point to hold the points of the child object.

Next, we loop for all the points of the child object and determine the two counters: depending on which parent is greater we adjust one of the two counters. Since all counters are integers any division between them will be cast to the closest integer. Then, in line 21 we extract the points of its parent throughout the counters and then multiply by the ratio in order to obtain the points of the child object.

The examples in Figures 4.21 and 4.22 illustrate the pursuit for in-between hybrid objects.

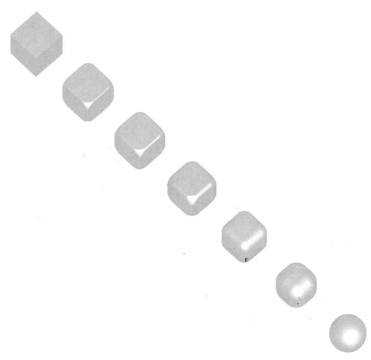

4.21
The mid-hybrid object may be defined as either a *spherical cube* or a *cubical sphere*

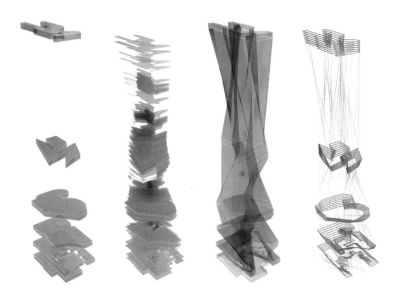

4.22
Vertical transitions (class project by J. Paek and C. Santos for course GSD2311 taught by Kostas Terzidis in Fall 2005 at Harvard University)

Endnotes

[1]MEL stands for Maya Embedded Language. It is a way of instructing Maya to execute a series of actions through commands typed in an editor. It is also referred to as scripting. The difference between scripting and manual design is in the complexity and unpredictability of the actions. The human designer may be constrained by quantitative complexity and may be unable to construct unpredictability since that would negate a designer's intellectual control.

In Maya the script editor can be invoked by selecting **Window->General Editors->Script Editor**.... A window with a divider should appear. The lower part (white) is where you type in the scripts and the upper part (gray) is the part where Maya responds to the scripts. In the menu bar at the top you can execute the scripts by selecting **Script->Execute** (or simply Ctrl-Enter). Help for each command can be found at the menu bar under Help.

A script is composed of variables, operations, and commands spelled and placed in a specific syntax. If the syntax or spelling is wrong, Maya will respond with a complaint (in the gray area of the editor). A free educational version of Maya is available at www.alias.com/maya

[2]The word *interesting* is derived from the Latin word *interesse* which means to be between, make a difference, concern, from inter- + esse (=to be). Interestingly, the in-between is literally interesting.

5 Amphiboly

An amphiboly is an ambiguous grammatical construction. It is a statement whose meaning is indeterminate in a peculiar way: while the statement has an obvious meaning it also has a hidden or concealed meaning. An amphiboly occurs when the construction of a sentence or the placement of an accent or punctuation allows it to have two different meanings even if all of its terms are clear.

An amphiboly is an equivocal construction so framed as to point distinctly at something while, at the same time, implying the existence of something else. It is an ambiguity that consists not only of the double use of language, but also of artfully winding into the mind ambivalent suggestions of an ambiguous nature without leading to any unique direct conclusion. It uses certain clauses, which can be so connected with other clauses as to divide the mind between different views or parts of the meaning intended.

The fallacy of amphiboly is caused by faulty sentence structure, and can result in a meaning not intended by the author. In contrast, allusions, innuendos, or insinuations are grammatical constructs aimed at intentionally implying imputations of an injurious nature to the character or reputation of the person referred to without making any direct accusation. Even though such expressions are indirect and subtle, they are usually derogatory in nature aimed at gradually and insidiously introducing a thought by subtle and artful means.

While amphiboly appears to be accidental it may also be constructed so as to appear to be as such. While the possibility of attaching an intention to a seemingly unintended statement implies suspicion, ill will or malice, the possibility of attaching unintentional sense to an intentional statement opens up a more intricate interpretation than has been previously possible.

Amphiboly differs from, but may be confused with, equivocation. Equivocation uses a single word to suggest multiple meanings, whereas amphiboly depends on the structural sequencing of words in a sentence, which can be interpreted in at least two ways with equal justification. Equivocation is based on the double use of language whereas amphiboly is based on the arrangement of words within a sentence. Therefore, an amphiboly can be defined as an equivocal grammatical expression when, taken as a whole, it conveys a given thought with perfect clearness and propriety, and also another thought with equal propriety and clearness.

The word amphiboly is derived from the Greek prefix *amphi-*, which means "on both sides" and the suffix *-boly* which means "stroke." The root of the word points to the existence of two opposite claims the contrast of which leads to a sense of suspicion not because of a lack of proof or quantity of information but because of the presence of contradictory evidence. It is a state of mind caused by the presence of antithetical clues that hinder the formation of a unique conclusion. While an amphiboly is about ambiguity, indefiniteness, and vagueness, it is also about duality, ambivalence, and coexistence. Rather than assuming two distinct states linked by an "either-or" relationship, a "both-and" relationship may occur instead. An amphibian, for instance, is capable of living both on land and in water. This property is caused by the integration of two distinct functions into one.

While the notion of opposition can be caused by the existence of two distinctly opposite points, it can also be caused by oscillation of one point between two opposite states. This possibility opens up a more intricate understanding of the notion of contradiction. Rather than assuming two distinct states linked by an "either-or" or a "both-and" relationship, an "in-between" ambivalent continuity may emerge instead. Such a case involves time as a measure of comparison between these antithetical states. The complementary duality of these actions ensures that for every pair of reverse actions the scene returns to any of its two states, as if nothing ever happened. For instance, a pendulum's swing back and forth can happen repeatedly and yet at any moment there are only two possible distinct states. This observation reveals a repetitive pattern of events where time is of no importance. Instead, the focus is set to the in-between time span when the swing is understood as potentiality. A folded sheet, for instance, is not understood as an isolated, independent, or complete object but rather as a hidden, latent, or virtual potentiality to deploy. Rather than approaching amphiboly as an operation of isolating opposites, it should be understood as the unification of a complementary pair, the importance of which lies "in between" as the one state owes its existence to the absence (or the possible existence) of the other.

An oracle is an ambiguous statement aimed at predicting a specific future event. It is an amphiboly expressed in the form of an enigmatic statement or allegory. For instance, the meaning of the oracle framed as "you will go and return not die in the war" depends on the placement of the comma before or after the negative word "not." If the comma is placed before the word "not," the phrase reads "return, not die." But if the comma is placed after the word "not" the phrase reads the opposite way as "return not, die!" Similarly, the oracle to King Cresus when consulting about a war with Persia: "If you cross the river, you will destroy a great empire." This he applied to the Persian empire, which lay beyond that river, and, having crossed, destroyed his own empire in the conflict. What is interesting about oracles is that they both affirm and negate the ultimate metaphysical questions about future and existence; by articulating a sentence in the form of an ambiguous statement, an oracle becomes a mind game, an enigma, the hidden meaning of which is to be discovered or guessed. At the same time, it uses a fault-proof hidden logic: as the only logical means of predicting future events is by utilizing an if-then hypothetical clause, an amphiboly cleverly incorporates also the alternative "else" within the same statement, pointing at both the assertion and negation of a possibility all at the same time. As such, an oracle provides an answer to any question simply because its formulation includes all possible and impossible scenarios.

An oracle differs from a prophecy. While an oracle is an answer to a specific question, a prophecy is a god-revealed prediction about the future. Oracles use logic as a premise

5.1
Pythia on her Tripod giving an oracle to a pilgrim (from the Vulci crater by the painter Codrus 440 BC)

to formulate predictions whereas prophecies deny logic. While an oracle may appear contradictory, opposed to common sense, or utilizing absurd terms, eventually it may be true in fact.

Just because one doesn't know something that doesn't mean that it doesn't exist. By the same logic, just because one knows something, it doesn't mean that it does exist. An inference is a process of deriving logical conclusions from premises known or assumed to be true. Thus, while a conclusion may be true, derived from a truthful, consistent, and valid inference, the premises it is based upon may be false. Because inference is a logical process, it is objective, universal, and traceable; yet the premises of an argument may be arbitrary. The problem with this is that arguments can be constructed whose logical consistency may appear to lead towards a truthful conclusion but whose premises are accidentally, inadvertently, or perhaps deceitfully false[1].

What makes amphiboly interesting for architects and designers is that it involves two fundamental principles of form: structural articulation and visual appearance. Ideally, visual appearance of a form is consistent to its structural logic. For instance, a tree is a structural system that has a formal visual consistency, and vice versa the formal manifestation of a tree reveals its underlying structural system. However, there are cases where the two are inconsistent or even antithetical. In other words, out of a multitude of different structural possibilities there are some that stand out merely because of a perceived discrepancy between their structure and their appearance. In particular, when the discrepancy is antithetical then the phenomenon is referred to as ironic. However, in all cases, the measure of discrepancy is based on the predicate assumptions associated with what structure and form is (or should be). This system of underlying premises is an important framework upon which evaluation, critique, and eventually acceptance are established.

Challenging these assumptions, an architectural amphiboly is an ambiguous formal construction. It is a form whose meaning is indeterminate in a peculiar way: while the form conveys an obvious meaning it also has a hidden or concealed meaning that is associated with its structure. An amphiboly occurs when construction, perception of attributes, i.e. light and shadow, or placement of viewpoint allows it to have two different meanings even if all of its structural terms are clear. An amphiboly is an equivocal construction so framed as to point distinctly at something while, at the same time, implying the existence of something else. It uses visual connotations, which can be so connected with other visual connotations as to divide the mind between different views of the meaning interpreted.

Order and disorder are assumed to be two fundamental antithetical conditions in architecture. Order is a term used to describe the condition of regular or proper arrangement; its absence, disorder, may denote an infinite number of antithetical arrangements. One case of disorder is randomness. Randomness is defined as the quality of lacking any predictable order, pattern, purpose, or objective. Instead of viewing order or randomness as two separate, distinct, and opposite states, it may be far more beneficial to study the process of transition from one state to the other. In such a way, both order and disorder can coexist within the same organization as one state emerges out of the gradual absence of the other. To illustrate the point an example is given: a grid-like structure transforms gradually into a convoluted scheme with numerous overlapping coils or folds revealing complex patterns. While the upper part may appear as weakening, or crumbling, or the disintegration of an orderly base, it can also be read as the result of a mutated alien order. The contrast of two different orders within the same structure allows the reading of an in-between zone where one order progressively transforms into another.

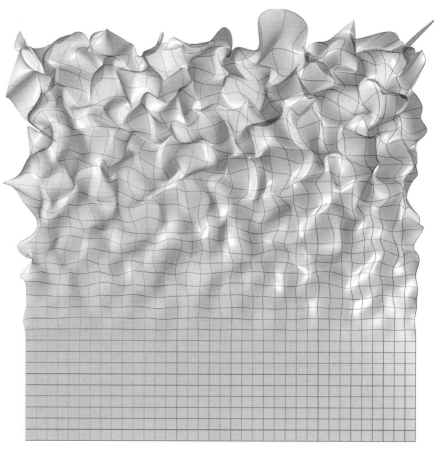

5.2
Entropy

(Syn) biosis

In biology, a parasite is an organism that grows, feeds, and is sheltered on or in a different organism while contributing nothing to the survival of its host. It lives in or on the living tissue of a host organism at the expense of it. The biological interaction between the host and the parasite is a type of symbiosis where two (or more) organisms from different species live in close proximity to one another, in which one member depends on another for its nutrients, protection, and/or other life functions. The dependent member (the parasite) benefits from the relationship while the other one (the host) is harmed by it.

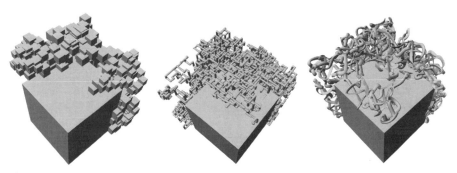

5.3
A cube (host) is taken over by various types of parasitical formations

In Figures 5.4 and 5.5, a fractal-based solid form is subtracted from a stack of cubes creating a void space. The boundary surface is used to extract the construction curves which then become visible as mullions. The void space becomes the atrium of a high-rise building hosting IRS services.

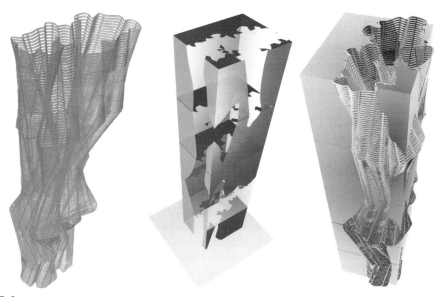

5.4
Lattice inscribing the void (left), subtraction from a stack of cubes (center) and final form (right)

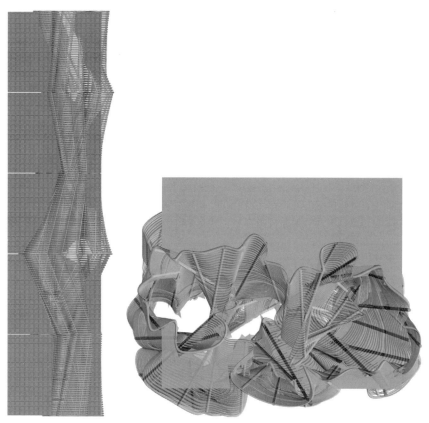

5.5
Elevation (left) and view from above (right)

En (dia) meso[2]

One of the main differences of morphing, as it compares to deformation, is in the *duality* of its identity. Deformation is understood as a change relative to an initial state. As a point of reference, an archetype is needed to assess the degree of deformation. However, as the deformation persists, form reaches a threshold beyond which it becomes "unrecognizable," meaning that it is impossible to associate it with its pivotal archetype. That is not the case in morphing. In fact, as the interpolation persists, the hybrid form oscillates between the identifiable shapes of its parents allowing comparisons to be made at any point. This formal atavistic property is very important, as it becomes a means of expressing change through form itself, and not through juxtaposition. The duality of its identity is a unique compositional and unifying theme of the hybrid form.

5.6
The hybrid is an implicit form that suggests a dynamic blending of genetic forces superimposed by the subtle reminiscence of its creators

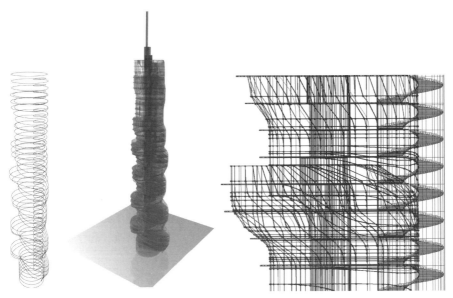

5.7
A cylinder is deformed based on site context (view and sun). Its deformation is captured in eight steps

5.8
Horizontal sections (left) of a 50-story residential high-rise (right)

(Syn) diasis[3]

Boolean algebra involves the partial order on subsets defined by inclusion, i.e. the Boolean algebra on a set A is the set of subsets of A that can be obtained by means of a finite number of the set operations union (OR), intersection (AND), and complementation (NOT). Boolean architecture is an accumulating process that results into intricate assemblies by combining elements progressively into increased complexity. In this context, a concert hall composed of a series of ellipsoid acoustical modules is presented as an example of Boolean algebra. The project illustrates not only the aesthetical potential of such operations but also the structural complexity involved (class project by Valerie Chatelet and Jean Hwang for course 2311 taught by Kostas Terzidis in Fall 2003 at Harvard University).

5.9
The envelope of the concert hall (plan)

5.10
The envelope embeds specific geometrical relationships between each member of the audience and the performers on the scene. Ellipsoid is the basic geometrical element. The foci of each ellipsoid are anchored on the stage and on one of the members of the audience. Each member of the audience becomes the seed of an ellipsoid that will reflect the sound directly on her/him. Once as many ellipsoids as members of the audience are created, a Boolean union operation was applied to extract the exterior surface.

Endnotes

[1]See Capaldi, N., *The Art of Deception: An Introduction to Critical Thinking.* Prometheus, 1987; Engel, M. and R. Steiner, *With Good Reason: An Introduction to Informal Fallacies.* Bedford, 1994; and Walton, D., *Informal Fallacies: Towards a Theory of Argument Criticisms.* Benjamins, 1987.

[2]The term ενδιάμεσο(pron. endiameso) in Greek means in between.

[3]The term συνδύασις(pron. syndiasis) is Greek and means combination. It is an operation between couplings, i.e. συν + δυας (=couple). The unit of the operation is a couple rather than a single element.

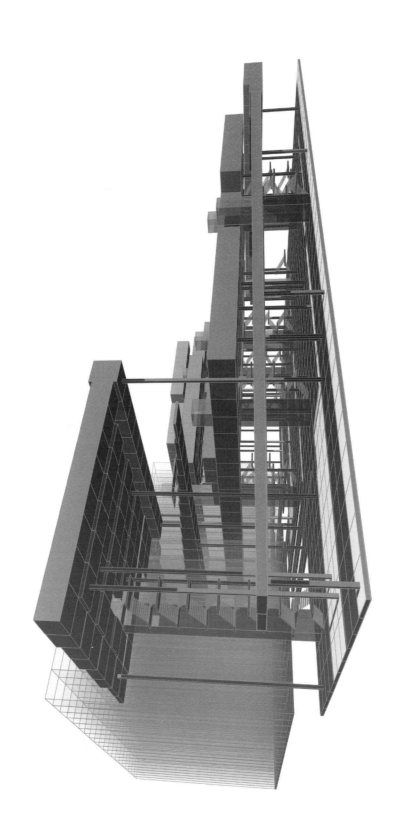

6 Periplocus

Complexity is a term used to denote the length of a description of a system or the amount of time required to create a system. While complexity may be a characteristic of many natural systems or processes, within the field of design the study of complexity is associated with artificial, synthetic, and human-made systems. Such systems, despite being human creations, consist of parts and relationships arranged in such complicated ways that often surpass a single designer's ability to thoroughly comprehend them even if that person is their own creator. Paradoxical as it may seem, humans today have become capable of exceeding their own intellect. Through the use of algorithms, computation, and advanced computer systems designers are able to extend their thoughts into a once unknown and unimaginable world of complexity. Yet, the inability of the human mind to grasp, explain, or predict artificial complexity is caused mainly by quantitative constraints, that is, by the amount of information or the time it takes to compute it and not necessarily to the intellectual ability of humans to learn, infer, or reason about such complexities. Because of its quantitative nature, the study of complexity involves by necessity computational methods as means of analysis, simulation, and synthesis of systems that involve large amounts of information or information processing.

The word *periplocus* is Greek and is used here to denote a special kind of complexity that is not based on the quantity of information involved. The word itself is composed of the prefix *peri-* which means *around* or *about* and the root *plocus*, which is derived from the verb πλέκω (pron. plehko) which means *to knit*. Through its etymological roots, periplocus refers to an indirect yet intentional activity of fabrication. While the closest English word that would correspond to the word periplocus would be *per-plexity*, it fails to address the connotative subtleties present in the Greek version: artificiality, indirectness, and simplicity. The difference is that the notion of periplocus involves human intervention as it can only apply to artificial objects or situations. Further, the notion of perplex involves intent to create confusion, trouble, or doubt whereas periplocus, while intentional, is not aimed at deceiving but rather at the emergence of a product or a situation that exhibits uncertainty. For instance, the labyrinth was a periplocus structure not because it had numerous windings or multiple path choices but rather because it could artfully disorient one using simple means. In that sense, it was periplocus because it was conceived by a human mind, had an indirect effect, and was simple. Contrary to complexity, periplocus involves simplicity as an underlying principle.

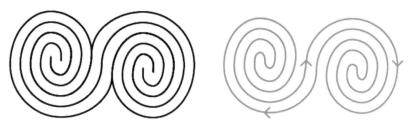

6.1
Possible structure (left) and path (right) of the labyrinth

There is often confusion between simplicity and significance. While simplicity may imply lack of sophistication, it also suggests abstraction, clarity, unpretentiousness, austerity, and straightforwardness. In contrast, complexity is often regarded by theorists as indicative of sophistication, novelty, uniqueness, originality, and advancement. Because of its intricate nature and its limited understanding, complexity is associated with superiority, mystery, extraordinariness, and rightness. In contrast, simplicity has often been "accused" of being too obvious, boring, uninteresting, and suspicious.

While complexity theory per se, as it applies to computation, cryptography, probability, or randomness, is by definition complex, the formal manifestation of these processes is, usually, straightforward. If there is computational complexity innate to mathematical models, it is not in their form but in their internal structure and behavior. Structural complexity is not necessarily an indication of formal complexity and, vice versa, formal complexity is not necessarily an indication of structural complexity.

Consequently, the frequent use of the word *complex* as a means of description of formal properties is not always an indication of superior understanding, expertise, or elitism but often a lack of one's ability to ensure and convey a sufficient level of expertise, command, and understanding of the subject. In such cases, the term *complexity* is used as a means of separation, demarcation, possession, or restricted access. In contrast, simplicity, regardless of its connotations, demonstrates clarity, approachability, and mastery of the subject.

The term algorithmic is often connected with complexity. While the objective or result of an algorithm may be complex, the strategy itself does not necessarily follow that complexity. In mathematics, it is common practice that a simple formula generates extremely complex outputs. For instance, chaos itself is the study of how simple systems can generate complicated behavior.

In the following examples, simple means are employed to create complex structures. The design strategies used are based on repetitive, stochastic, or distributing algorithms that while abstract and universal exhibit various degrees of uncertainty, perplexity, and intricacy in their final architectural formation.

Recursion

Recursion (or *anadrome* in Greek) is a term used to describe a process in which the definition of an entity refers to the entity itself. For architecture recursion is an ontological process that involves the existential formation of infinitely nested structures through self-replication. Such processes have a unique structural and aesthetic architectural value, since they incorporate generative strategies that encapsulate self-resemblance; the rules that produce the whole are the same rules that produce the parts. As an example a series of fractal-based daedaloid trails is shown in Figure 6.2. The algorithmic logic that

6.2
A series of recursive fractal-based daedaloid trails

produces the complex pattern is quite simple: a process that creates a curve is recursively called so that the curve does not intersect itself and re-tracks itself when the intersections are so many that the system runs out of space.

Subtle rotations

Iteration or epanalepsis[1] is a process of repeated performance of an event. It is invoked by executing the same set of instructions a given number of times or until a specified result is obtained. In architecture iteration is employed as an ordering device that produces repetitive patterns. Such patterns suggest the presence of motion, change, or progress as a visual impression.

An ambiguous algorithmic structure for a house of worship uses fields to create transparency out of solidity and at the same time has the ability to camouflage its interiority through rotational repetition (class project by Andrew Saunders for course GSD 2311 taught by Kostas Terzidis in Fall 2003 at Harvard University).

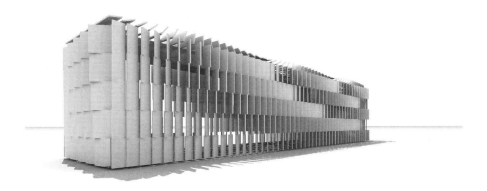

6.3
The result of the algorithm is an ambiguous figure that creates transparency out of solidity and at the same time has the ability to camouflage its interiority

Stochastic search

Stochastic search is a process in which building elements are placed at random locations in space that are then evaluated against a set of constraints to be accepted if there is a satisfying fit. The random search space can be adjusted to match the zoning envelope and the con-straints can match structural, circulation, or programmatic requirements. In this particular problem a simple program of 200 residential units (50 1-bed 900 sq. ft, 100 2-bed 1200 sq. ft, and 50 3-bed 1600 sq. ft) was to be placed within a 70 × 70 ft. site (class project by Julie Kaufman and Brian Price for course GSD 2311 taught by Kostas Terzidis in Fall 2004 at Harvard University).

Programmatic distribution

A stochastic search is utilized here as the core algorithm for allocating programmatic spaces within a given site.

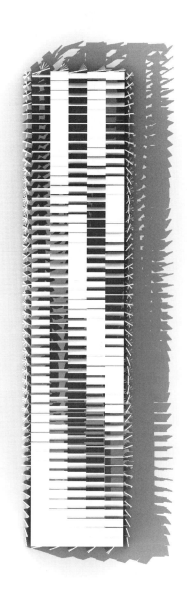

6.4
Top view

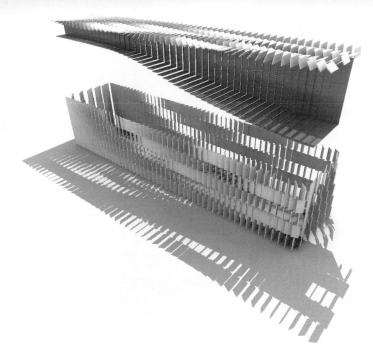

6.5
In this image the bottom part is the original field and the top separator allows the parti and program to emerge

6.6
Elevation views

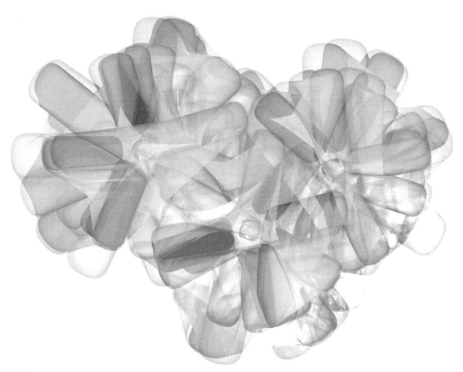

6.7
View from above

6.8
Horizontal sections: interlocking tower plans

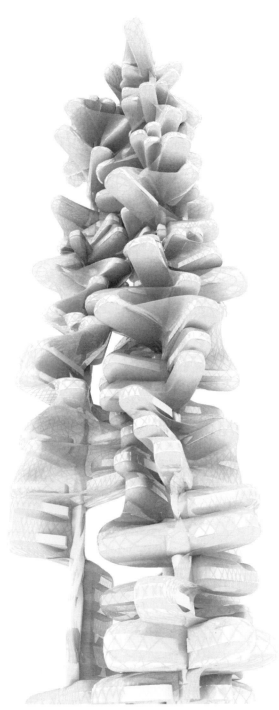

6.9
View upwards from the ground

The program includes spaces, subspaces, square footage, and required links to other spaces within the program. The program for a small 7600 sq. ft library is shown below:

Public Library

Main Entrance			**1000**	links to Exit Control
Exit Control			**1000**	links to Main Entrance
Book Circulation			**1500**	links to Entrance
Circulation Processing		500		
Circulation Desk		400		links to Exit Control
Shelving	100			
Supply	200			
Office	100			
Stacks		600		
Periodicals			**1000**	
Stacks		500		
Reading		500		links to Exit Control
Reserve Dept			**200**	
Reserve stacks		200		
Reserve Desk	100			links to Exit Control
Office	100			
Reference			**800**	links to Exit Control
Stacks		500		links to Exit Control
Public Toilets		300		
Interlibrary Dept			**700**	links to Exit Control and Ref
Office		100		
Reserve Desk		400		links to Exit Control
Processing		200		
Technical Processing			**1100**	links to Exit Control
Acquisitions		300		
Workroom	100			
Bookkeeping	200			
Staff Toilets		300		
Catalog		500		
Bibliography	150			
Cataloging	250			
Office	100			
Administrative			**300**	
Offices		300		links to Catalog
Director		100		
Associate Directors		200		

$$\overline{}$$

7600

The algorithm employs an XY coordinate system that generates a square range to accommodate available positions for the program units. The architectural programs of a library could be satisfied by accumulating a certain number of such modular units, each of which has its uniqueness in X and Y values as a spatial entity and its Z value is determined by the connectivity between each other. So in one program and its subprograms within, or in several programs which share their intimacy, their Z values will be the same thus architecturally being placed on the same floor level. Otherwise, they will be at different levels and connected only by the vertical circulation

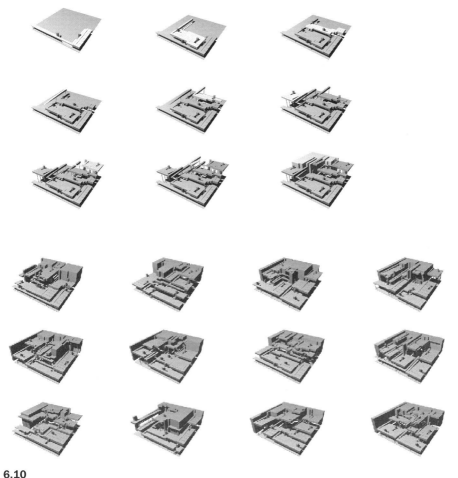

6.10
Steps in the process of allocating program spaces recursively within a 30 × 30 unit square site

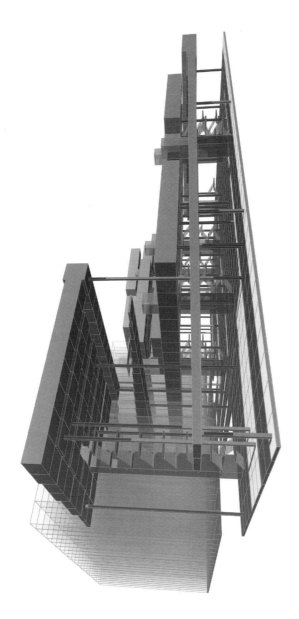

6.11
View of the emerged library

equipments (VCE), a program with its maximum number of connections that interlink every level. An algorithm applies the above rules, starting by selecting one unit and then an agglomeration of direction is chosen randomly so as to provide multiple solutions and flexibility for the program specifications.

To further enhance the quality of the model as a building, each position on the coordinate system is evaluated as to whether to put columns, or a set of VCE, or to open up as entries, etc. – a reference layer is created upon which each unit represents positions on the coordinate system. By certain algorithmic rules, their Z values are determined and once they reach a designated number, which is set as a "Yes" answer to the program's criteria, it will execute these steps repeatedly in order to add more architecture elements to the model. In the last step, all the reference units on the activated positions will be moved into Z by −1 as to finish the model as its building basement (class project by Xu Zhou for course GSD 2317 taught by Kostas Terzidis in Spring 2005 at Harvard University).

Endnotes

[1]*Epanalepsis* is a Greek word that means "to say or do what one said or did before." It literally means receive over again.

7 Epi(multi)logue

1. NEW

Kostas Terzidis
04:21am
Oct 16, 2005
GMT-0500 (8.1)

In Chapter 1 under the title "The strive to capture the elusive" I presented the argument that "nothing comes out of nothing and nothing disappears into nothing" which, if true, signifies an inability to achieve something out of nothing, i.e. to create something new.

Kei Takeuchi
03:43pm
Oct 16, 2005
GMT-0500 (11.)

The argument in the context of novelty may well lie in a rhetorical question. Basically, I agree with that "nothing comes out of nothing and nothing disappears into nothing." Of course, we could say that everything comes out of nothing and everything disappears into nothing. Or nothing comes out of everything and nothing disappears into everything. However, it sounds like a paradox. Even though someone invents something new, it consists of some substances. Also, one can make any sentences or meanings; however, they are deemed to have words that have already existed. That is to say, the paradoxical argument of novelty may not transcend the boundary of its linguistic nature.

In a magician's show, a magician is likely to emphasize "nothing" before showing his trick; however, nobody believes there is nothing; moreover, revealing a trick is one of the most intriguing parts in a show. In this sense, they seldom think of a magic as novelty. If a magician liked them to do that, he would call it an illusion. Interestingly, David Copperfield's website offers many definitions of magic. Among them, the last word is illusion: 1. The act of creating the impossible; 2. To defy mother nature; 3. To reappear; 4. To levitate; 5. To suspend disbelief; 6. The art of making people dream; 7. Making fantasy a reality; 8. To fly. He likes to call his magic an illusion; however, it is certain that he just pretends to be able to do that. And then people are likely to think of his magic as novelty.

When it comes to the term design, we can say that it is not only the vague, intangible, or ambiguous, but also the strive to capture the elusive in languages. However, the term design is attributed to rhetorical expressions as well as to the act of designing itself. Specifically, like a child, one starts to create something new before knowing the term design. Sculptors deal with forms when they design. Painters deal with colors when they design. The linguistic expressions can be said to represent and reinterpret our reality, but they are not our reality itself. This gap may lead us to the argument in the context of novelty.

At last, I'd like to add a passage from Albert Camus: "Why am I an artist and not a philosopher? Because I think by words and not by ideas."

Kostas Terzidis
07:22pm
Oct 16, 2005
GMT-0500 (11.1)

Your argument is quite interesting. The interplay of words in a sentence may reveal new concepts. However, I would be skeptical in attributing the concept to the linguistic game, but rather assume that the concept already existed; it was the right combination of words that revealed its existence. For instance, in magic we have two points of view: the trick (a concept or process conceived in advanced) and its presentation (an articulation to deceive the audience). If you are able to decipher the right articulation you may be able to see the truth which was already there. Uncovering the truth requires trusting your logic rather than your senses.

James Steel
04:18pm
Oct 16, 2005
GMT-0500 (12.)

I am willing to concede, that "novelty," and "new-ness," are more precisely used to describe transformations than objects. Where I take issue with the material, as it has been presented, is that it seems that etymology has been hijacked to serve the theory that a "new" kind of architectural process, practice, design, creation, etc. cannot be put into words. The use of etymology to espouse the elusive ends up resulting in semantics and self-indulgent conclusions that "new" words must emerge or that language can simply not describe, represent or participate in, creativity. To say it simply, the belief (I use the word belief because the word theory seems vague) is based on no word appropriately describing "new" because "new" does not exist. As I said, I'll give you that "new" probably is not most accurately used to describe objects, but a whole lot of ideas have been "new" to me and I'm going to keep using the word "new" to describe them.

Architecture, like all the arts, is at once engaged in preservation, observation and maintenance of language (communicative vocabulary of form and logic) and yet at the same time architecture is an act of invention, ingenuity and imagination (Kostas' last paragraph) that transcends and transforms language. There are examples in literature that might make this more apparent.

James Joyce, I think we can all agree, used language in a "new" way. (Note: I am using the word new to describe the act of writing.) His work was both engaged in a system of language and yet, dare I say, original and inventive in the way he used language.

To relate this back to the material presented, design is both participatory in a language and emergent from that language. This is what makes it elusive. Kostas most clearly expresses this elusiveness in the illustration where logic (perceived order) and irregularity (perceived disorder) are seen as either and both, ambiguous, yet in transition. For this reason, I am uncertain if Kostas meant to infer that fashion emerges from design's "starting point." In the first full paragraph of the last page he wrote: "Because of its investigative nature, design is always associated to a starting point, a pivot, out of which style, fashion, or mannerism results." I would argue that fashion is elusive, as Wes notes once something is fashionable it is no longer. Fashion does not result from design's reliance on a starting point, because that would mean that fashion has a starting point. Rather, design propagates fashion's elusiveness by no two designs ever starting from the same point. And each point is "new!" Mannerisms, on the other hand, are not a part of fashion, per se. Mannerisms have more in keeping with observation of a language or decorum. These are the forces that both enable fashion and yet constrict its desire for absolute novelty. Fashion can be thought of as the "trace" famously defined by Derrida. It has no beginning (starting point) and no end, and can only be traced.

When Eisenman wrote that "modernism hadn't begun," he did not simply mean to suggest, as Rowe and others had, that the "Modernists" (Le Corbusier and others) had not made a clean break with the past. He was also inferring that no architectural style is ever, or can ever be, entirely "new," in isolation or autonomous. "Modern," and "New," are aspirations and desires not their resulting objects. Mark Wigley's writing on the "fashioning of modernity" might best describe the history of the modern movement's fashioning.

Kostas Terzidis
06:31pm
Oct 16, 2005
GMT-0500 (12.1)

The purpose of challenging a word is not to eliminate it but rather to detect, establish, or perhaps, re-establish its true meaning. The use of etymology is simply a means to trace its original meaning so as to detect potential deviations that may or may not reflect its true meaning. Instead of assuming that a change in meaning of a word is simply the result of a natural evolution, I tend to be a bit more skeptical about its intended use. If, after challenging, a word is found truly to be indeed in the path of an evolution into something else, then fine. But if there is the slightest doubt then it needs to be investigated further. Maybe then perhaps new, pneu, or gneu (or whatever it is named) will cease or continue to be an aspiration or a desire.

In Martin Heidegger's words: "Words and language are not just shells into which things are packed for spoken or written intercourse. In the word, in language, things first come to be and are. For this reason too, misuse of language in mere idle talk, in slogans and phrases, destroys our genuine relation to things." See Heidegger, M., *Introduction to Metaphysics*. New Haven: Yale University Press, 2000, p. 15.

James Steel
11:24pm
Oct 16, 2005
GMT-0500 (12.1.1)

I'm not sure what you meant by the "true" meaning of a word. I guess that I am skeptical of searches for "truths" because such searches tend to arrive at perceived origins instead. If I am to understand you correctly, you are arguing for a Saussurian structuralism of linguistics. I would like to think that contemporary theory has moved beyond Saussurian structuralism where a one-to-one relationship exists between signifier and signified. Lacan's description of schizophrenia broke down Saussurian structuralism.

From Frederic Jameson's essay "Postmodernism, or The Cultural Logic of Late Capitalism":

"Very briefly, Lacan describes schizophrenia as a breakdown in the signifying chain, that is, the interlocking syntagmatic series of signifiers which constitutes an utterance or a meaning. His conception of the signifying chain essentially presupposes one of the basic principles (and one of the great discoveries) of Saussurian structuralism, namely the proposition that meaning is not a one-to-one relationship between signifier and signified, between the materiality of language, between a word or a name, and its referent or concept." (72)

Jameson goes on to describe how meaning (and the signifier) is now free to move from signified to signify. The signifier is now manifest of a "meaning-effect" and each signifier's signification is a product of the generative and projective meaning given in its relationship to other signifiers. The "snapping" of the signifying chain leads to a sea of lost signifiers, without relationships to a signified. The issue thus becomes not how a "chain of signification" can be re-constituted or re-constructed, but how the signifier can move freely from the referent in the present, constituting meaning in its relationships to other signifiers.

To say this more simply, I don't think that you can go back (in the case of language). I entirely agree with you that a word can, and should, be traced and interrogated for its origins, its history. But this does not reconstitute a word's "meaning." If it has a "meaning," it is entirely based on its current connotation, its relation to other words. This is how one can use the word "new" for the communication of its relative meaning rather than an absolute.

While I like some of Heidegger's writings, I don't agree with his understanding of language. One could argue that Joyce "misused" language. Yet I would not say that Joyce "destroys our genuine relation to things." In fact, one of the few places that novelty (the "new") emerges is in "misuses."

Kostas Terzidis
11:47pm
Oct 16, 2005
GMT-0500 (12.1.1.1)

While the origin of a word does not reconstitute its meaning (I agree with you), it does serve as a reference to detect the original meaning. In doing so one is able to see the natural, accidental, or controlled subtleties.

I am afraid that detecting the meaning of a word based on current connotations may be futile. You yourself admitted that the current use of the word new is not entirely meaningful, i.e. certain uses of it are not entirely accurate and that another word should be used instead. Why? Why not keep using the word new "as is" since that is its current connotation? What if the connotation is wrong? How do you trace its falsity?

James Steel
05:18pm
Oct 17, 2005
GMT-0500
(12.1.1.1.1)

I think that the "origin" of a word is as elusive as its current connotation. As I've tried to explain in previous postings, the material (spoken or written) word is just a signifier. Signifiers, one could say, are ever-changing, not just now but always. As many post-structuralists have said, the word "dog" could just as easily mean "cat." There is no "truth" to the signifying chain of signifier to signified. This does not mean that signifiers (words) are insignificant or that their use should not be precise. It just means that there is no "truth" to their use, now or before. And "precision" does not mean a "right or wrong" (or true or false) use, but the use of a word with an intention and an understanding of its current relation to other words.

Etymology is a fascinating study. When I said that I felt it was being "hijacked" I meant that etymology works as a "trace" but not as a way to ensure, preserve or resurrect any "truth" to the signifying chain of a word (signifier) to its meaning (signified). If anything, etymology assures us of an extant transformation of language (and architecture), a kind of continual becoming. And rather than directing creative thinking toward absolute and eternal truths, I would prefer that efforts were directed outward. To quote Deleuze, as everyone else does: "lines of flight." Meaning, for knowledge to expand, and for creativity to occur, novelty must be an inevitability. Desire and aspirations should be ambitiously pursuing the unattainable, the inconceivable, the unimaginable (impossible?), etc.... the new. For without acts of singularity and individuation we will not know what is possible.

The idea that nothing is "new" does not serve the provocation and promotion described above. It begins to sound exclusionary and nihilistic. One could as easily formulate an argument that "all is new" as has been argued that "nothing is new." But, like Deleuze and Guattari's "war machines," such kind of thinking must be fought vigilantly.

Matthew Snyder
09:24pm
Oct 16, 2005
GMT-0500 (15.)

Dictionary definitions tell part of the story of a living language. In fact, dictionary revisions are based on citations and comparisons from preeminent writers and academics in order to arrive at a (rational?) contemporary (new?) definition of a word. Thus using a 2000 year old definition of a word as evidence of a more "true" definition is about as convincing as using a 2000 year old tool to show the capabilities of a tool from the current age. The story is useful, but the definition cannot be taken with mathematical precision. In a leading academic environment, our responsibility should be to lead the dictionary definitions of certain concepts rather than follow them. The question remains: is the latest definition of a word new? And is anything new?

The discussion of innovation and discovery prompts a short dip into the history of physics:

The notion that there is nothing new in the world is indeed supported by modern science. A cosmological story which postulates quarks, leptons, and assorted subatomic particles as the basis for all matter agrees that these particles have been around since cosmological origins and before, and have participated in universal transformation only in their re-combination. There is no allowance for spontaneous genesis of new matter. Further, no information exists without occupying space and matter. Every word spoken, thought considered, byte stored on a computer, occupies some assemblage of molecules in space. If the matter is the same, are the thoughts the same?

(This prohibition of spontaneous genesis in fact is not a consequence of scientific thought, but at its heart. It is forbidden, in rational scientific method, to resolve a problem with a wave of the hands and "poof!". This is tantamount to relying on God. This is actually quite an interesting line to pursue in itself, since the relationship between science and society as a whole is especially strong in our era.)

Yet, in Galileo's cosmology, quarks, leptons, and assorted subatomic particles did not exist. Thus the story "we" tell of his time is different than the story "he" told of his time. Science is a mental construct developed and applied to that which we experience as physical reality. Newton "discovered" gravity. It was a pre-existing force around which he was able to formulate predictive equations.

So the story goes. Yet Einstein reformulated the predictive equations of gravity. It is not a force, he said, it is curved space. Einstein's equations using the curvature of space replicate our measured universe with far more accuracy and precision than Newton's force based model. Does gravity exist? Do we know what it is? Was it preexisting and discovered? Something keeps us from spinning off the surface of the earth and into space, yes. We can calculate and predict with precision what will happen to an object moving in this environment. Slightly closer to architecture, the concept of force is essential to the most basic engineering problems. We trace them through building structure. We draw force diagrams. Yet the leading physicists of our day can only propose inconclusive theories as to what exactly a force might be. Our understanding is forever bound up in the intellectual constructs we use to explain the world we experience.

Ours is a layered existence that rarely encompasses direct experience of the universe. To the extent one has a direct experience of reality one might call that experience essentially not new – or conversely – eternal, there is no difference when experience transcends the construct of time (one gets strangely close to the irrational which science long ago excluded).

On the other hand, to the extent that our experience is supported on layers of developed constructs, the possibility of the new is continual, and is part of the complex development of academic thinking.

Architecture itself is enmeshed within these layers. To even define this word would result in much sophisticated bantering among professionals. But the above leads to the conclusion that architecture is primarily representation and persuasion, the wielding of Jefferson's mighty pen. In practice, the ability not just to conceive of a "good" design (leave aside the problem of evaluation for a moment), but the ability to "persuade" a board to proceed with construction of the design is at least equally important.

To return to the problem of evaluation, while intuition and a sense of what's right or wrong may often lead a designer in a certain direction regardless of whatever rational methods are currently being taught, and while that sense is probably related in a complex way to the ideas circulating in society at that time, it is the designer's ability to develop a persuasive argument for the design – one that fits within the ideas circulating in society and further develops them – that will allow the design to live or die. It is the ability to locate the work intellectually within the discourse – the development of the construct – that defines the work as architecture. Perrault said architecture exists only in the mind of the designer and has no connection to the natural world. Twisting his meaning slightly in the light of the above, I would agree. Architecture, in any form, is a political act before it is a physical one.

Martin Wellnitz
09:46pm
Oct 16, 2005

Given that design "is about conceptualization, imagination, and interpretation" in contrast to planning which "is about realization, organization, and execution," the etymological, seemingly to the past referring interpretation of the word as "something we once had, but have no longer" could also be understood as the strongly temporary character design has.

The thought making the design manifest cannot be foreseen and is thus to be referred to in the past tense.

"Innovation" in relation with "audience" complemented by space or place seems to be of importance. Nowadays, in the information age with real time communication, information can be spread over the whole globe within seconds and reaches people at every place at the same time, whereas in past times information had to be spread from person to person with space as the retarding. So things were introduced as being new, although known at the place of their initial appearance for quite a time.

Defining the "new idea" as the result of looking at existing elements leads to the conclusion that there is nothing new. What is important when thinking about the new is to think about analyzing and taking apart the existing system, part, or principle and then combining the parts to something that didn't exist before. Thus the new evolves from the old combined with (human) ingenuity.

Therese Tierney
11:05pm
Oct 16, 2005

One of the important points made in this essay seems to be the distinction between planning and design. Planning is concerned with logistics and execution, with risk-management and "the known." Design is something more complex, operating as a nexus of an entire set of cognitive, social, and physical activities.

Design contains what Terzidis calls "the unknown or unre-membered." As such, the design process doesn't repro-duce or represent a pre-existing idealized Platonic form, but instead acts as an emergent tendency operating within field dynamics. According to Deleuze, "The field, however, does not preexist, but is always present as a virtuality. Determined within and by the plastic events that articulate it and render it actual." Therefore, what is intrinsic to design is always present, but it may exist as a virtuality, or an unre-membered unknown. While the genesis of an architectural idea is its own contextual reality, as Terzidis explains, the interactive space of ideas results in a reordering of realities. Here again, we might find agreement between Bergson's concept of emergence as "making itself in the process of differentiation," and Terzidis' "reordering" as it were.

We could further argue that there is no tabula rasa in design. Seen from this perspective, design acts are not just predictable formalizations of thought into spatiality (i.e. planning), but operate within a modal continuum of actuality. While the contextual field is pre-existing, the process of unpredictability, that "what we don't know yet" occurs through a reordering and expressive becoming-other.

Jason Kerwin
02:32am
Oct 17, 2005

The idea that the "new" can be so easily converted into "novelty" is counter-intuitive to the nature of "newness." Re-framing the architectural production within the realm of cultural norms appears to give the sense of the "new" but on further inspection, the strategies are generally less than original. But is this really the issue? Successful artistic production was not so interested in establishing the "new" more than a perceptual understanding that grew from contextual references. Minimal art was not "new" in the manners of representation but the position within the gallery, relationship to the viewer, and subsequent serial production was considered "new."

This is not a concept that should be argued from an etymo-logical point of view. Jacques Herzog recently articulated, within the context of Modern architecture, Le Corbusier wrote extensively and yet the writing is useless without the buildings themselves.

In a way, the argument is not so relevant within architecture due to its drawn out period of gesticulation. Fashion works in much faster and much larger fields of popular culture which thrives on the "new" and establishes its value within the market-place based upon the length of a season. Ironically, the "new" in fashion is simply the re-working of a past design, but the fashion world has a very short memory.

Innovation is a different term altogether in the sense that it can be quantifiably measured. In today's terms, the performative nature of the building can be accurately predicted, simulated, and constructed. Innovation is not reliant on a "new" material but merely the considered response to a set of parameters. Again, the innovation comes from the differentiation from baseline conditions.

Kostas Terzidis
07:23am
Oct 17, 2005

Herzog (in his debate with Moore) makes a quite revealing statement: he says that he (and his partner) did not seek to create forms or patterns. They were there. He just discovered them, and as such, they speak for themselves.

As Herzog makes constant reference to Rossi, his teacher, as a source of inspiration the connection becomes even clearer: it is about the archetype, origin, archaic, and unexpressed that they are both seeking.

Christian Santos
09:14pm
Oct 24, 2005

I remember reading once how Michelangelo believed the same things about his sculptures (which he favored over all other art forms). While many would claim divine inspiration, he would say that his sculptures already existed in the block of stone he was carving. All he was doing was revealing them. I suppose you could still connect that to divine inspiration. Either way, one should take a good deep look at his "unfinished slaves."

2. Impossibility

Kostas Terzidis
07:25am
Nov 17, 2005

If there is a possibility, however remote it may be, there must be a chance that it will occur. While the human mind may be bounded to the limitations of quantitative complexity, its computational extension, the computer, allows those boundaries to be surpassed. The notion of "impossible" is no more the assessment of human imagination but rather a degree of probability.

Matthew Snyder
04:56pm
Nov 17, 2005

Well, let me just return for a moment to the question of whether it is possible to calculate ALL the possible combinations of pixels in a relatively low resolution 2D image.

The image was something like 135×180 pixels or so, don't remember exactly. And we figured that meant something of the order of $1 \times 10 \char`^ 7000$ possible combinations.

Given that guesses at the total number of atoms in the universe, for instance, are something like $3 \times 10 \char`^ 90$ atoms, $1 \times 10 \char`^ 7000$ is just too big to work through here on planet earth. While I believe in the advantages of using computer power, immense as it may be, to iterate dumb repetitive tasks, there are still numbers, easy to conceive of, that are impossible to arrive at practically.

Just imagine how we would produce those $10 \char`^ 7000$ iterations:

I'll give you 7 billion computers, one for every person on earth. And let them all operate at 10 G IPS. And let's see how long it takes to process $10 \char`^ 7000$ instructions.

10 G processor $= 1 \times 10 \char`^ 10$ iterations/sec

$60 * 60 * 24 * 365 = 3 \times 10 \char`^ 7$ sec/year

$(3 \times 10 \char`^ 7$ S$)(1 \times 10 \char`^ 10$ IPS$) = 3 \times 10 \char`^ 17$ iterations per year for one computer

multiply by our parallel processing power of 7 billion computers, and we get

$(7 \times 10 \char`^ 9)(3 \times 10 \char`^ 17) = 2 \times 10 \char`^ 27$ iterations per year.

We still have $10 \char`^ 6973$ iterations left. That year's work could be absorbed in a rounding error. And these processors have been working around the entire globe for the whole year. No one has done any other work. It's actually been a pretty fun year, we've all been outside enjoying each other's company.

But let's imagine we develop quantum computing to its theoretical maximum and we can push our 7 billion computers from a measly 10 G to 100 trillion G. That's pretty big, right? Faster than Deep Blue, and far surpassing the human mind. And say we can do this speed on a scale of 7 billion computers. That means we get to add just 14 zeros to our $2 \times 10 \char`^ 27$ iterations per year and come up with $2 \times 10 \char`^ 41$.

So with this unlikely number of unlikely powerful computers, we now have 10^{6969} instructions left. We will be done in about 170 years if there are no power failures or wars.

We must also consider that this is an incredibly low resolution two dimensional pixel grid that started this whole process. If we are thinking three dimensions and finer resolution, add a few hundred or few thousand more zeros to the exponent, and what do you do with them?

I have a question. If you still think this is in the realm of the possible, would it be okay for me to present for my final project, a modeling script beautifully conceived and yet, due to the potential for organized complexity and emergence, impossible to fully evaluate, and tell you that the results will be so meaningful and unexpected that they will blow all our minds, but that, unfortunately, the project is so cutting edge that the computer is still calculating and it is difficult to tell in how many years it will be finished?

All in good humor, but I am curious how you can still say "possible" in the face of numbers like this. (Your previous response was that either it is achievable, which the above seems to refute, or that adding intelligence to the searching routine to "learn" patterns as it goes will arrive at the solution – which is both true and useful, but cutting down on the iterations is an admission that the large number of iterations is untenable.)

Kostas Terzidis
11:41pm
Nov 17, 2005

I guess you are right...

Maybe then it is futile, albeit not impossible. The fact that we are even talking about a (remote) possibility is indeed a definition of possibility itself; otherwise we would not be able to talk about it, would we not? However, as an alternative to futility, let's assume that not all possibilities are equal. Certain possibilities may have a higher chance of success than others. This possibility of possibility opens up a more intricate relationship than has been previously possible. Rather than going mindlessly through all possible patterns in search for the lucky one, we can instead evaluate each random step. By assessing the degree of promise that a certain pattern has the notion of selection is introduced in the random process. The selection starts with a finite group of completely random patterns. In each step, the degree of promise (or fitness) of the random pattern is evaluated, multiple patterns are stochastically selected from the current group (based on their fitness), modified (mutated or recombined) to form a new pattern, which becomes current in the next evaluation. This process is referred to as a genetic algorithm. For example, using the previous example, instead of assuming that each random pattern is equal in importance and therefore going through all of them until a perfect match has occurred, a preferential selection may occur instead. The number of iterations in the case of Icarus will be reduced quite significantly from $10 \wedge 7669$ to merely 3,280,000.

In brief, blind randomness won't take you as far as being a little bit smart. But then again what is smart?

Ultimately the issue of impossibility involves human judgment. The real reason of concern here is not whether impossibility exists as a possibility (i.e. if you can think of it, it exists) but rather about whether we as humans are in control of the concept. I tend to believe that Matthew's and my frustration with the zeros is not really about the zeros (i.e. the degree of precision) but rather about our fear of losing control of that concept to some-body else. How can it be that such an alien to us, hard to grasp concept (that of $10 \wedge 7000$) can possibly be a simple routine concept for somebody (or something) else. Who is that thing? Should we be alarmed?

Matthew Snyder
01:58pm
Nov 19, 2005

Where are the boundaries between thinking, being, and doing? Are there boundaries?

Interestingly, the question of the possibility of artificial (or machine based but real) intelligence in computers is based solely on speed. The binary framework of simple gates that underlies computation today doesn't seem to be as much of an issue. Quantum computing theorizes a more continuous condition, based on the vascilations of a probability cloud, but I think much of that discussion is also focused on how to pull a definite yes or no out of an uncertain system. We are again up against the issue of human need for predictability.

A programming language, the binary machine language upon which it is built, the hexadecimal transposition which makes this machine language easy to manipulate in the hands of an engineer, the extreme rationalism of mathematics, the zero and the base system (base 2 base 6 base 10) are all theoretical conceptions of the mind that seamlessly translate into the practical space of ordering beans on a table, or calculating the partitioning of property through the stock market. Did they start in the mind, or start on the table of beans? Or is there really no difference?

If someone programs a random number operation into a script and chooses the formal result she sees on the screen, is she exercising a different type of authorship than someone who accidentally drops a few sticks into an architectural model and becomes captivated by the new architectural possibility it suggests? Setting aside the legal sense, can anyone ever really make a claim to the creative genesis of a design?

Kostas Terzidis
03:24pm
Nov 19, 2005

Random numbers may possess the same degree of unpredictability as stick throwing if outcome is the criterion for comparison. Yet, this type of unpredictability is not based on the materiality of the medium used but rather on the intellectual mechanisms involved. The term *intellectual* entails the capacity for knowledge and understanding. While certain activities (i.e. open color aquarelle, throwing sticks, etc.) are initiated through intellectual intention to pursue new knowledge, the materiality of the medium used is not of an intellectual nature. Material events, such as chemical changes (i.e. bleaching, burning) or physics-based events (i.e. throwing sticks, crumbling paper), may be unpredictable yet are certainly not intellectual. In contrast, the computer as a medium has indeed intellectual characteristics as it entails the capacity for knowledge and understanding. Its ability to uncover unpredictable events is based on its active logical mechanisms and not on passive observable chemical reactions. While that may not matter if the objective is merely the outcome (as they both look alike), it does indeed matter if one is interested in the origins of unpredictability and its true nature.

Matthew Snyder
09:13pm
Nov 19, 2005

So a computer uses the physical properties of material (silicone, etc. and electrons running around) to represent a purely rational conceptual system which is developed by the mind. Yet the means of the representation (zeros and ones represented by discrete voltages) is of such a resolution that the chemical or mechanical properties of the material do not affect the representation. You're calling that intellectual. (I feel another discussion in there....)

The mind uses, as far as the academic world is generally concerned, a randomly evolved assortment of firing synapses that, I'm guessing, occur at a resolution which is dependent upon the chemical properties of the material from which they are formed. If that is the case, would you call the mind unpredictable yet certainly not intellectual?

The other question is a quantum computer which relies on the material qualities of an uncertain electron cloud to represent this rational conceptual system. If a quantum computer was to actively use this material quality, does this mean the quantum computer is also not intellectual?

In other words, is materiality really the issue, or is the issue the presence or not of a logical, rationally based system that can be translated exactly into a functioning (and fast moving) material counterpart as in a computer?

Kostas Terzidis
12:37pm
Nov 20, 2005

In response to your argument I will attempt to shift away from the scientific realm and try to address it within the context of design:

I think the issue we are examining here is whether design thought is quantifiable? In response to this question, two options appear to be possible: either that design is a process based upon finite elementary units, such as bits, memes, nodes, atoms, etc. or that it is a holistic process with no beginning, end, or any in-between measurable steps. The negation of discreteness implies a continuity of thought that permeates throughout the process of design but is confined within the boundaries of human domain. By definition, subjectivity depends on interpretation and only humans are in a position to do so (yet). Certain intellectual activities, such as intuition, interpretation, choice, or meaning are considered human qualities that can hardly be quantified, if ever. In contrast, the discretization of design opens up a multitude of possibilities as it invites discrete mathematics to be involved in the design process, such as logic, set theory, number theory, combinatorics, graph theory, and probability.

Discretization of design by definition can be addressed, described, and codified using discrete processes run today by discrete numerical machines (i.e. computers). However, the problem is that discrete/quantitative design provokes a fear of rationalistic determinism that is long considered to be a restraint to the designer's imagination and freedom. Such resistances have attempted to discredit Computer-Aided Design as inadequate, irrelevant, or naïve. Design is considered a high level intellectual endeavor constructed through uniquely human strategies (i.e. intuition, choice, or interpretation). Such theoretical design models negate the computer as a possible source of design conceptualization mainly because it is based on discrete processes that are finite and as such restrictive. In contrast, human thought is continuous, infinite, and holistic.

Ramona Albert
05:28pm
Nov 20, 2005

This topic that we are discussing is in a sense never ending, and disputable to no limits. Computers have allowed us to transcend into a world that is reminiscent of the Platonic Cave, a space where reality intersects the human imagination. Computers in their existence are nothing but machines that operate on a series of rules. These rules do not give them any trace of intellect but pure mechanical properties based on human manipulation. I am not sure about the capabilities of the computer for design conceptualization, but I am confident in using the power of these machines towards the benefit of implementing a concept. "As intellect is to opinion, so is science to belief, and understanding to the perception of shadows." The world generated by these machines is a way of visualizing the "shadows" and their constructability.

Christopher Shusta
09:26pm
Nov 21, 2005

Why shouldn't intuition be able to be replicated by a computer? Isn't intuition just a natural result of the composition and networking of our brains? Someone like Wolfram might argue that the physical world is not continuous, but made of discrete elements. If matter (and thus a human brain) is in fact discrete, then it follows that it is quantifiable and (like the pixelated painting) replicable. Akin to the discussion that keeps coming up, it seems highly improbable, but is it impossible?

3. Tool?

Kostas Terzidis
02:38pm
Nov 27, 2005

The word *tool* is often used to describe the synergistic interaction of designers with computers. A tool is defined as an instrument used in the performance of an operation.

The connotative notion of a "tool" implies control, power, dominance, skill, and artistry. A pen, for instance, is a device that allows one to perform or facilitate the manual or mechanical work of writing or drawing. The capabilities, potency, as well as limitations of a tool are known or estimated in advanced. This is not the case with computers. Neither their capacity or potency is understood, nor their limitations be pre-estimated. Indeed, designers are frequently amazed by processes performed by algorithmic procedures, which they have no control or, often, knowledge of.

Maher El-Khaldi
12:46am
Nov 27, 2005
GMT-0500 (3.)

I believe if someone claims that a design drawn by a pencil is his or hers for they used it to draw, then a design generated by algorithms, computers, hammers, sticks, etc. is also his or hers for they generated those rules, or spent an effort, for it to happen, etc.... now, let's look at this: when we set up a proportion system of geometry for a building, we are simply taking one thread from a big net that has millions of relationships... thus, the deeper we dig into those systems, the more findings we will acquire be it: relations, proportions, rules, etc.... and yet we call those our designs, because we say it is a rich system that we set up thus any finding we have is a result of our design... same case with a pencil... the only difference is that you don't have much of the attributes other than the tip, angle, how rough or fine, and yet these help generate unlimited design possibilities... just think "calligraphy" ... it is all based on those variations of pencils tips... the only difference is that these are so obvious they make us believe that we know how to control it... thus we know everything about it and we can claim everything coming out of it... but when a tip breaks, and suddenly generates a certain form of a tip due to some extra force exerted by the painter's hand, he or she can find a new stroke type, etc.... now when it comes to computers, it is just the same... so I think it is an endless dilemma to discuss design in terms of ownership in relation to tools....

I believe that when we design, we are only taking some parts or pulling some threads of bigger interconnected networks of relationships... and we always seize the moment and try to utilize what we know of, but will we be always late as things are ahead of us... but that does not make us any less designers than we are.. if we use a computer or a pen, design in part is a continued seizure of chances, possibilities, abilities, skills, tools, etc.... from there I would argue any design happens because I started it, and therefore it is mine. Now, there are many directions that this design can take but one is for sure: that I initiated it!

Kostas Terzidis
02:38pm
Nov 27, 2005
GMT-0500 (3.1)

I agree with you except you have to keep in mind that there is a thin line that separates pencils from computers: design is an intellectual activity. While certain activities (i.e. open color aquarelle, or smudging) may have initiated through intellectual intention, the materiality of the medium used is not of an intellectual nature. Material events, such as chemical changes (i.e. bleaching, burning), or physics-based (i.e. stick throwing, pencil tip breaking) may be unpredictable yet are certainly not intellectual. In contrast, the computer as a design tool implementing processes such as randomness, stochastic, or recursion has indeed intellectual characteristics. Its ability to involve unpredictable events is based on its active logical mechanisms and not on passive observable chemical reactions.

Ramona Albert
07:33pm
Nov 27, 2005
GMT-0500 (3.1.1)

I must agree that computers are nothing more than just simple tools that implement the thoughts of the designer (by that I mean a human being). Computers are indeed tools, simply because they don't have a mind of their own. The fact that a computer can implement processes such as recursion, stochastic etc. does not define intellectual characteristics. The capability of computers to do these processes is simply mechanical. Just as a cell phone rings when someone is trying to reach us so a computer simply knows what to do because it is programmed. Imagine if computers really had a mind of their own, then we would be living in a nightmare where we had no control over them at all. Even when working with algorithms we need to be in control of our designs. The act of design cannot be simplified to only that of drawing a building. Design implies one's thought process, mood, attitude, points of view, soul…, etc. a computer is not programmed to exhibit such things and it remains a simple tool.

Junfeng Ding
09:42pm
Nov 27, 2005
GMT-0500 (3.1.1.1)

I agree with you. As a tool, I don't think there is much difference between the computer and any other tools that we are using; and I have to admit that no matter which tools the designer chooses: pen, watercolor, or computer, the accidence and randomness somehow will happen and can be part of the creativity in the design process. I guess people are more random than computers are. There are thousands of stories that we are familiar with, like how to create a new recipe by accidentally putting something wrong into a food.

The intelligence of the designer relies on how successful the handler controls the tools in order to transform accidence to be a piece of creativity with a sense of aesthetics. Since the tools don't have any feelings, the design result represents the designer's artist ideas and spatial imaginations.

Christopher Shusta
11:09pm
Nov 27, 2005
GMT-0500 (3.1.2.1)

Granted the two approaches are similar in many ways, but I think you're missing the point. The difference is not in how these tools (I hate that word) are used. The difference is on a more fundamental level: decision making.

Drawing is a mode of representation. CAD is a mode of representation. Scripting things like logical loops, constraints, and cause–effect relationships is not so much a mode of representation as it is a mode of generation. There is a key difference between channeling an idea into a form (through the conventions of physical drawing, computer drawing, physical model, computer model) and channeling a process into a form (something scripting seems to facilitate nicely).

I do not mean to imply that scripting as a design process is superior to doing it the conventional way, but it is most definitely different at its core. Conventional architectural design is all about making decisions from the top down (you make the big decisions and continue to make residual decisions based on what you learn) while scripting seems to bias the role of human decision making to a more bottom-up approach (you define some base parameters and let the computer make the big decisions).

So, when used in this manner, the computer is not equivalent to the pencil. The pencil is never actively generating form, only representing the designer's idea of it. The computer, however, can theoretically act as a decision maker.

If you've ever done an algorithmic project, you may have noticed that you can't approach it in the same way you normally would an architectural project. Already, at the base of your design decisions, your thinking becomes radically different. Again, not better, but different. In fact, my bet is that algorithmic skyscrapers will be spectacular failures, but the thinking behind how to design them will be an interesting change of pace.

Matthew Snyder
12:47pm
Nov 29, 2005
GMT-0500 (4.)

It's useful to understand that a pencil is productive in design because of its place as a component of a larger design methodology. Plan drawings, section drawings, and the notion of scale, for instance, are all powerful rational concepts which underlie and help to drive "pencil" based design. When translating an idea between physical built form and represented form, the ability for a designer to move ideas on paper between scales and modes of representation is made possible through a more or less rigorous adherence to a rational system which has been developed over centuries of design.

Just as my grandmother has great difficulty knowing what to pay attention to on a website filled with deceptive banner ads and pop-ups as well as useful content information, someone unfamiliar with the system of representation will not understand what the pencil is doing to facilitate design. Without a comprehension of the system, the representation loses much of its content and design information.

Renaissance perspective construction is another example of a system within this system. This is a purely rational mathematics and geometry based system for the translation of representation, developed in conjunction with pencil and paper representation.

Jon Conway's simplification of Von Neumann's cellular automaton is similarly a rational mathematical and geometrical based system. His publication of what was called the Life game in Scientific American of 1970 prompted an avalanche of graph paper and pencil explorations into what the system could deliver. The rationale behind the explorations differs from explorations into, for instance, perspective construction, in at least a couple of ways. Perspective has primarily been used to represent "something" preconceived. Not the case with CAs. Also, the rigor with which the rational system is employed is often not so critical, in general, with perspective geometric explorations, whereas it is understood to be extremely critical, essential in fact, in the case of cellular automata explorations.

But this is not always the case in design. Scott Cohen's designs, both pre-computer and post computer, are based exactly on a critically rigorous adherence to the rules of a geometric system, which is allowed to generate, allegedly, an "unpreconceived" logical geometric result.

These are all ideas which developed under analysis and experimentation with rational, human developed, systems. As it turned out, both renaissance perspective construction and cellular automata logic required very little translation to be applied within the logic of a computer. One could argue, in fact, that it was the humanist love of rational systems which produced the experimentation which led to computers.

Computers brought speed, speed which is now used to iterate human logic through unprecedented numbers of loops. Wolfram's greatest discovery (despite what he will tell you about himself, and independently of mathemetica) may well be the effect of CAs at extremely high resolution – something only possible with computers (and a heavy dose of insomnia), but based entirely on human logic.

Speed may at some moment in the future bring us the rational, controlling, and seemingly psychologically motivated HAL. This seems to have already happened in the narrow bounds of a master chess player and chess playing computer. Speed may bring us the moment in Planiverse when a human programmed 2D creature suddenly speaks a word that was not programmed into its lexicon. But it's not clear that, outside of a well constructed fictional world, we will feel this is intelligence.

Is a sense of intelligence equivalent to proof that there is intelligence? Is it possible to ask that question without a priori believing in a logical system? Is there an independent, non logically based means to verify intelligence?

To those uninitiated, sufficiently advanced technology is indistinguishable from magic (Arthur C. Clarke). Does magic exist?

At this point in history, I have not yet turned on my computer, or sat down after letting it run for several weeks, and found something unexpected – unless I had programmed something into it and (ironically) "expected" something unexpected. I have found things on my computer that were programmed by someone else and came from my web link to appear on my computer – and in this sense the whole internet network may have a more powerful potential for dramatically providing something unexpected in the future.

But in this sense, I probably come down on the side of the computer as machine shop: useful for creation of tools, but not yet providing anything back to me that wasn't the expected or expectedly unexpected result of an a priori human system.

Kostas Terzidis
01:42pm
Nov 29, 2005
GMT-0500 (4.1)

Programming is a way of conceiving and embracing the unknown. At its very best, programming goes beyond developing commercial applications. It becomes a way of exploring and mapping our own way of thinking. It is the means by which one can extend and experiment with rules, principles, and outcomes of traditionally defined architectural processes.

In developing computer programs, the programmer has to question how people think and how mental processes develop and to extend them into real dimensions through the aid of the computers. In other words, computers should be acknowledged not only as machines for imitating and appropriating what is understood, but also as vehicles for exploring and visualizing what is not understood. The entire sequence of specifying computer operations is similar (albeit not equal) to that of the human thinking. When designing software, one is actually transferring processes of human thinking to a machine. The computer becomes a mirror of the human mind, and as such, reflects its thinking.

Some time ago I was at a conference that investigated the future of computers in Architecture. I had expected that the panelists would address the opportunities presented to architects and designers alike by the advances in computer aided research. Instead, almost everyone seemed interested in exploring existing programs, as opposed to holding a philosophical position driven by their own concepts... At that time I asked a question to a panel of experts about the necessity of designers to know how to program computer code. The answers that I got from them were very surprising to me, ranging from "what does programming have to do with design?" to "yes, design applications should be customizable." At that point I realized that the question should have been "how much programming should the designer know?"

You may already have deduced that I do think that programming is an important part of design education and practice. Programming involves more than simple problem solving, because it is the only way to use the computer to its full capacity, and for challenging known facts. Programming is the vehicle for obtaining new knowledge, for seeing things that cannot be seen, and for taking your fate, as a designer and architect, in your own hands.

Let me give you an example of a personal experience. This example deals with the very basics of architecture: perspective and three-dimensionality. As we all know, any CAAD program will allow the designer/architect to project into space any object/point, and will be able to render it accurately, as long as the designer/architect does not challenge the very basis of the architectural projection: that of a projection being always bound to a formula of positive numbers.

For example, the mathematical formula for a perspective projection is $f(x,y,z) = (x*t, y*t)$ where $t = d + d/z$ and d is the distance of the user to the projection surface. What if I give d a negative value? Can you imagine what that would look like? Can you draw the result on a piece of paper? (it is just a simple formula, isn't it?) Do you know of any CAD application that would allow you to mess around with the perspective projection? I doubt you would find any such application unless somebody gives you the application's code for you to change. But that would involve two things: the designer/architect knowing how to program and the developers giving them the code.

In reality, there is an unraveling relationship between the needs of a designer/architect and the ability of a specific program to address these needs at all times. This can be attributed to a number of factors. First, designers are never really taught how to program (one needs to look no further than the question/answer "What does programming have to do with design?"). Schools do teach students how to use CAD tools, how to play around with applications, but they do not venture into teaching the language, structure, philosophy, and power of programming.

Secondly, CAD developers rarely release code. You will be asked what you want, you will be offered interfaces for customization but you will not be given access to the code. For good reasons, code is proprietary information, and information is power. So, if a designer/architect wants to mess with the perspective formulas, they will need to write the modeling, interface, display, optimization, and debugging modules on their own. How many people who either have the time or the know-how to do this do you know? When are we going to see a Linux-like CAD system? When are we going to start a community of designers/ architects/programmers sharing common code, for the advancement of CAAD?

I tend to believe that now, a designer/architect's creativity is limited by the very programs that are supposed to free their imagination. There is a finite amount of ideas that a brain can imagine or produce by using a CAD application. If a designer/architect doesn't find the tool/icon that they want they just can't translate that idea into form. And whenever they see a new icon (let's say "meta-balls") they think they are now able to do something cool. But are they really doing anything new? If a designer knew the mathematical principles and some of the programming behind the newest effects, they would be empowered to always keep expanding their knowledge and scholarship by always devising solutions untackled by anybody else. By using a conventional program, and always relying on its design possibilities, the designer/architect's work is sooner or later at risk of being grossly imitated by lesser-devised solutions. By cluttering the field with imitations of a particular designer's style, one runs the risk of being associated not with the cutting-edge research, but with a mannerism of architectural style.

In this light, there are many designers claiming to use the computer to design. But are they really creating a new design? Or are they just re-arranging existing infor-mation within a domain set by the programmer? If it is the programmer who is asking first all the questions, who is really setting the parameters and the outcome of a good design? We saw already the I-Generation (Internet-Generation). When are we going to see the C-Generation (Code-Generation) – the generation of designers/archi-tects that can take its fate into their own hands?...

Acknowledgment

This is to thank all the people involved in these dialogues for their insights and great ideas. While the purpose of this dialogue was to seek a diversity of opinions, some of the contributing people's original comments may have been corrected grammatically, syntactically, and slightly altered.

Index

Alexander, C., 35, 51, 60, 62
algorithm, 15–17, 19–23, 25–7, 30–31,
   38–41, 43, 57–9, 65–6, 85–6, 88,
   94, 119, 121, 127, 129, 144, 148
algorithmic, 2–7, 20, 23, 31, 37, 41, 57,
   59, 65, 119, 121, 129, 148, 150
allo, 23, 32–3
ambiguous, 1, 16–17, 37, 48, 53, 105–7,
   109, 121, 132–3
amphiboly, 53, 105–9
antithetical, 2–4, 6, 17, 56, 106, 108, 109
archetypes, 9, 11
array, 72, 74–5, 89, 90–3, 96–7, 101
attributes, 74

Bataille, G., 11, 13
black box, 42
Blue Gene/L, 18
Boolean, 43, 60, 80–81, 114–5

CAD, 24, 28, 37, 41, 47, 54, 61, 150,
   154–5
cellular automata, 94, 98, 151–2
Chronos, 10
complex, 22, 41, 52–4, 88, 94, 96, 109,
   118, 119, 120, 138–9
complexity, 16, 23, 27, 29, 37, 38, 43, 45,
   51–3, 55, 62, 94, 103, 114, 117–9,
   141, 143
computational, 17–18, 21, 23–4, 26–7, 29,
   34, 38–41, 45–6, 52, 54–60, 65,
   117–18, 141
computer, 15–29, 33–4, 37–44, 45–7, 49,
   52–62, 117, 137, 141–155
computerization, 57–8, 62
conceptualization, 1

conscious, 16, 23, 25–6
continuity, 28, 38, 56, 97, 106, 146
contradictory, 2, 106, 108

Dada Engine, 22
Dadaist, 21
data types, 68
Deleuze, 56
design, 1–2, 4–8, 12, 19, 20–29, 37–56,
   58–62, 81, 94, 103, 117, 119, 132–3,
   138–141, 145–155
determinism, 28, 51, 147
digital, 22, 39, 40, 54–6, 62
discovery, 7, 8, 22, 24, 33, 35, 137, 152
discretization, 28, 146
duality, 106, 112

Eisenman, 34, 54, 58, 61, 63, 134
emergence, 1, 6–7, 10, 40, 55, 94, 118,
   140, 143
Epimetheus, 10
etymology, 1, 132, 134, 136
Euclidean, 8, 62
existence, 1–3, 5–8, 12–13, 18,
   23–4, 32, 53, 55, 105–7, 109,
   132, 138, 147

fashionable, 7, 133
feedback, 9
finite, 15, 28, 29, 42–3, 48, 54, 65–7, 94,
   114, 146–7, 155
flip-flop, 9
fractal, 48, 49, 88, 90–91, 93, 111,
   119–20

Gehry, 40, 53, 58
Godel's, 32
grammar, 21, 22, 48
grammatical, 21–2, 38, 105–6

Haraguchi,A., 18
Hegel, G. W. F., 11
heteromorphic, 99
heuristic, 45, 46
humanism, 56–7
humanistic, 23, 26, 55–6
hybridization, 97

Icarus, 30, 144
illusion, 5, 12, 50, 131–2
imagination, 1, 7–8, 18, 27–9, 41–2, 133–9, 141, 147, 155
impossible, 5, 7, 17–19, 23–4, 26, 29, 31, 35, 38–9, 46, 107, 112, 131, 136, 141–3, 147
incompleteness, 1, 32
infinite loop, 66, 87
innovation, 2–4, 53, 137, 139, 141
intellectual process, 23
intellectual property, 27
intelligence, 20, 31, 34, 35, 46, 58, 143, 144, 150, 152
intention, 25
interpolation, 99
intuition, 28, 42, 50–3, 57, 59, 138, 140, 146–7
invention, 7–8, 13, 15, 19, 22, 24, 48, 55, 133
iteration, 120

Koch, von, H., 48
Kuhn, T. S., 63

labyrinth, 118
language, 2, 6–7, 13, 16–17, 19, 22, 34, 40, 46, 50, 59, 61–2, 81, 105–6, 132–4, 135–7, 144, 154
linguistic, 2, 12, 15–17, 22, 24, 31–2, 34, 38, 45, 48, 131–2
loop, 66, 70–71, 78, 83, 85–7, 90, 92–3, 95–7
Lynn, G., 34–5, 55–7, 62

mannerism, 8
McLuhan, M., 34
memory, 2, 8–11, 47, 95, 141
metaphor, 32, 35, 50–51, 53
mind, 4, 7, 8, 11, 13, 15–21, 23–9, 31, 37, 41, 43, 52, 54–6, 58, 60, 105–7, 109, 117–8, 139, 141–2, 145–6, 149, 153
modern, 5, 134, 137
morphing, 49–50, 97, 98, 112

new, 2–8, 11–3, 16, 18, 20–22, 26, 30, 34, 39, 40–43, 48, 50, 54, 59, 65–6, 67, 83, 86, 94, 131–141, 144–5, 148–9, 154–5
newness, 4, 140
novelty, 2, 4–5, 7, 12, 118, 131–3, 135, 136, 140
NURBS, 40, 56, 58, 73, 74

Oedipus, 11
operations, 68
oracle, 107, 108
origin, 1–3, 5–6, 8–12, 23, 40, 73, 89, 90, 92, 135–6, 141
originality, 3, 4, 53, 118

Palladio, A., 21
paradigm shift, 54, 59, 63
paradox, 2, 6, 10, 12, 17, 131
parasite, 110
Parmenides, 5, 7, 11–3, 33
periplocus, 117–8
petaflops, 18
phenomenological, 55
phenomenon, 11, 53, 109
Picon, A, 60
planning, 1, 61, 139
Popper, K., 34
pre-Socratic, 5, 6, 12, 17
primordial, 1
programmer, 19–23, 27, 45, 54, 153, 155
Prometheus, 10

random, 21–2, 29–31, 66–7, 69, 76, 79, 82, 84–7, 96, 121, 143–5, 149
randomness, 18, 21, 27, 31, 55, 65, 76, 80–1, 109, 118, 144, 149
recipe, 65, 149

recursion, 18, 55, 119, 149
repetition, 70–71
representation, 12, 26–7, 32, 56, 59, 67,
    138, 140, 145–6, 150–51
reversion, 3
Rossi A., 11

scheme, 1
shape grammars, 48, 61
signified, 18, 134, 135, 136
simulation, 8, 45, 47, 54, 58, 117
stochastic, 15, 19, 84–5, 88, 119, 121, 149
strategy, 17, 19, 29, 37, 119

tool, 20–23, 25, 34, 38–40, 43, 47, 52, 54,
    56, 58–9, 137, 147–50, 153–5
transformations, 63, 73, 75, 97, 132

Ulysses, 32
unambiguous, 16
unimaginable, 27, 52, 117, 136
unknown, 12, 15, 27, 32, 34, 38,
    40, 52, 56–7, 67, 69, 117,
    140, 153
unpredictable, 21, 23–5, 27, 38–9,
    53, 67, 145–6, 149

vague, 1, 15, 40, 58, 132
variables, 67–8

Yessios, 49, 61

Zeno, 5, 12